RETHINKING
CATHOLIC
DEVOTIONS

ENERGY, ENGAGEMENT, TRANSFORMATION!

JIM CLARKE

Paulist Press
New York / Mahwah, NJ

Cover image by coldsun777/Shutterstock.com
Cover design by Joe Gallagher
Book design by Lynn Else

Library of Congress Cataloging-in-Publication Data
Names: Clarke, Jim (James J.), author.
Title: Rethinking Catholic devotions : energy, engagement, transformation! / Jim Clarke.
Description: New York : Paulist Press, [2022] | Includes bibliographical references. | Summary: "A wide-ranging discussion of popular devotionalism as practiced in the U.S. Catholic Church, with brief history of how devotions arose and ways to rethink them for the 21st century"—Provided by publisher.
Identifiers: LCCN 2021008367 (print) | LCCN 2021008368 (ebook) | ISBN 9780809155330 (paperback) | ISBN 9781587689307 (ebook)
Subjects: LCSH: Catholic Church—Prayers and devotions—History. | Devotional exercises. | Spiritual life—Catholic Church. | Catholic Church—United States—History. Classification: LCC BX2177.5 .C53 2022 (print) | LCC BX2177.5 (ebook) | DDC 242/.802—dc23
LC record available at https://lccn.loc.gov/2021008367
LC ebook record available at https://lccn.loc.gov/2021008368

ISBN 978-0-8091-5533-0 (paperback)
ISBN 978-1-58768-930-7 (e-book)

Published by Paulist Press
997 Macarthur Boulevard
Mahwah, New Jersey 07430
www.paulistpress.com

Printed and bound in the
United States of America

To all those faith-filled individuals who helped me to develop and deepen my faith over the years: my parents, teachers, friends, and saints from every walk of life who have accompanied me on my journey

CONTENTS

Preface vii

1. Devotionalism: An Affair of the Heart 1

2. History I: How Did It All Start? 7

3. History II: How Did We Get to Where We Are?...................17

4. Saints: Friends in High Places 29

5. Mary: A Woman for All Seasons 41

6. Eucharist: What Was Jesus Thinking? 57

7. The Passion: It's about Life, Not Death 69

8. Potential Problems: Watch Your Step!...............................81

9. Mature Devotionalism: Growing Up in Our Thinking 93

10. Into the Future: Move On!...107

Appendix..119

Notes..125

Bibliography...133

PREFACE

Devotionalism is a jewel in the life and culture of the Catholic Church. It might be described broadly as the ritualization of the heart's longing for connection with, and intercourse between, the devotee and the Divine. This desire of the heart expresses itself even further, to the personal attributes of Jesus, (e.g., mercy, love, wisdom, etc.), to Mary, and to the saints. As a "jewel," it must find its place in a particular setting—a setting that supports, enhances, and adds luster to its beauty. At the same time, however, the jewel owes much of its beauty and its attraction to the setting within which it is purposefully placed.

The practice of popular devotion belongs within the larger setting of Catholicism and has both the privilege and the responsibility that accompany that belonging. It has a duty not only to coexist with but also to actively participate in streams of developments in theology, learning, and spirituality. Ideally, it lives at the heart of the Church, not on its periphery. It is an enduring phenomenon, stretching back into the early history of the Church, but flourishing, especially in its Marian form, after the Reformation, and acquiring new and evolving manifestations over the past five hundred years.

Over the years, numerous writers have described and advocated particular Catholic devotions, often through the lens of catechesis. As a result, the faithful have been able to understand both the background and the ritual or prayer practice of these devotions, and large numbers of people have become emotionally engaged with them, in both private and group contexts.

There are, however, some cautions. This heartfelt approach to a faith expression can, and often does, become unmoored from its proper setting—the broader and deeper tradition of the Catholic faith. Specifically, it can, and too often does, fail to authentically engage the cognitive aspect of our faith: the centuries of scholastic learning, ongoing developments in theology, and a genuinely rounded approach to spirituality, informed by discernment and faith education.

As a result, devotionalism frequently becomes a source of comfort, rather than a tool for transformation. At its best, any devotion should generate a deepening experience of God that is translated into an active response of justice. In other words, the experience of love is meant to move us to the responsibilities of love.

In this book, I respectfully address the broad topic of devotionalism in the Catholic Church—its implications for a mature spirituality in individuals, and its impact on the ecclesial community. I do this by examining a variety of well-known Catholic devotions across cultural lines to probe the truth and meaning of each of these lines of faith expression. I explore the benefits—and the potential traps—inherent in many of these devotions and in devotionalism in general. When the historical and cultural context of a devotion is ignored and is directly applied with no discernment process, distortions can and do occur.

I address this book primarily, but not exclusively, to pastoral leaders in the Church, to assist them in their ministries and apostolates in their care for the faithful. I also hope that interested "people in the pews" will find it helpful, providing some new insights into the devotional life and marking out the pitfalls of an overly devotional approach to the faith that ignores the need for a sound intellectual respect for the larger tradition of the Church.

Using various insights from the fields of theology, depth psychology, anthropology, and spirituality, I explore the historical narrative behind a number of popular devotional practices and survey the principles of the ritualistic expression of their prayer practices. Informed by Church doctrine, I address the misconceptions, superstitions, misapplications, and misalliances behind some of these devotions. A strong linkage can often be discerned between faith expression and national origin; this gives space to a strange mixture of political and ecclesial influences and often leads to a cultic following. My intention is to separate the weeds from the wheat, so to speak, to help reclaim the original fire of the creator of the particular devotion.

Finally, I offer some helpful and healthy devotions for the present historical context. Making a case for the need for an embodied and prophetic spirituality, I then re-present much-loved devotions through that lens. These tools for adaptation will be clearly spelled out and accessible to anyone seeking to deepen and enrich their engagement with the Divine.

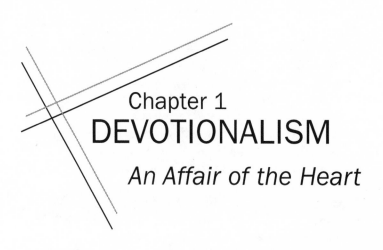

Chapter 1
DEVOTIONALISM
An Affair of the Heart

Like many Catholics, I grew up within the protective embrace of a deeply held religious culture that was supported by a thriving parish community and school system. Daily family Rosary and personal prayer fitted into an ongoing pattern of weekly Eucharist and monthly confession. In my teenage years, I became a member of the Holy Name Society and the Parish Charismatic Prayer Group. My parents had introduced me to the Charismatic Renewal, and it was in this setting that I experienced a profound encounter with God's love for me. This experience has empowered me and propelled me into a life that I had never dreamed of. To this day, I have lived my life out of that experience. It led me to the seminary, to priesthood, and to the pursuit of studies in theology, spirituality, psychology, and education, driven by a deep desire to invite others to their own encounter with Christ.

Through my adolescent years, this drive led me to leadership roles in the parish prayer group as a youth minister and retreat leader. The intimacy of my relationship with Jesus deepened, as did my involvement in the Church. I could not seem to get enough of the opportunities this experience gave me. I began the practice of reading the Bible daily and reading books about spirituality. In my daily prayer, I experienced a growing receptivity and intensity of God's love for me. I am eternally grateful for the devotionalism that brought me to this experience and that sustains me to this day. Without this beautiful gift, to which I was introduced by my parents, my journey of faith would not have the riches with which it has been blessed. I have learned what Pope Francis has stated before: "When Christ is the center of your life, everything else falls in its proper place."

Webster's Dictionary defines *devotion* as "deep affection, loyalty, piety, or enthusiasm for a person or activity."[1] This, in turn, is underscored by the dedication of time, energy, or money for that particular purpose. Within the spiritual framework, this then becomes the heartfelt expression of a particular connection with an aspect of spiritual inspiration of a person (e.g., St. Francis of Assisi or St. Catherine of Siena), place (e.g., Lourdes or Rome), object (e.g., Rosary or medallion), or event (e.g., Pilgrimage, World Youth Day, etc.).

A good image for devotionalism is fire. This symbol is energetic, engaging, and transformative. Several mystics have used this metaphor to describe their great love for God and the reason for their service to others. We often speak of people filled with the fire and power of the Holy Spirit.

Devotionalism as a phenomenon is the quality or state of one markedly characterized by religious devotion or practice. A practice can involve physical presence, action, or repetition of an emotional attitude. Simply put, it is a way of expressing our faith through the imagination and our emotions. However, one size does not fit all persons.

There are many reasons for this type of attraction, depending upon our family and cultural background as well as our own personality. Metaphorically speaking, the soul of each person has an underground natural spring that nourishes and supports the whole person. This could take the form of a particular discipline, prayer form, or devotional practice. When we collaborate with God to construct a conduit to tap into this spring, it can nourish a broader field of the soul. This is the purpose of spiritual practices or devotions—to sustain us over the long haul of human life with its many vicissitudes and challenges.

The following are some potential benefits of devotionalism:

- It fills an emotional gap that may be missing from our conscious life.
- It appeals to a particular personality type.
- It fulfills the desire for a mystical experience of God.
- It offers emotional comfort.
- It helps the practitioner to connect with a particular aspect of the Christian mysteries (e.g., Pentecost or Good Friday).
- It offers the individual an opportunity to go deeper into the emotional connection with a particular aspect of the Catholic faith (e.g., the Eucharist, the Rosary, Mary's role in the Church).
- It provides a link to the lives of the saints or to a particular saint.
- It offers a sense of belonging to the larger community (the Body of Christ).
- It gives a sense of bridging between the human and Divine.
- It allows us to create our own pious practices and liturgies of faith.
- It offers promises of real results either through hearsay or anecdotal accounts.
- It offers a feeling of control, in that devotions usually are characterized by a simplicity of words and form.

Devotional literature itself generally is not intellectual. It is not meant to be doctrinal or theological in the strictest sense. It seeks to engage our emotional and intuitive faculties, to give some measure of comfort, and, importantly, to move us to action. In the words of the United States Conference of Catholic Bishops (USCCB), "Devotions are expressions of love and fidelity that arise from the intersection of one's own faith, culture and the gospel of Jesus Christ." Such religious observances have been an enduring feature of the Catholic tradition and generally, when a popular practice remains alive and well over many centuries within a tradition, it is a reasonable proposition that it is meeting a genuine human need. Devotions connect the heart or emotional life to the soul; thereby transforming the interior life, which, in turn, challenges us to image more closely the God of infinite love and mercy we have encountered. Devotion is not just a private matter; it has tangible effects in the world.

A truly devotional person welcomes and collaborates with life.[2] Their religious piety is meant to move them beyond an impulsive idealism that burns out in the face of conflicts and life challenges. Creative thinking must form an essential core of devotion; otherwise love turns into sentimental enthusiasm that realistically serves no one.

This is borne out in the Directory on Popular Piety and the Liturgy:

> Genuine forms of popular piety, expressed in a multitude of different ways, derive from the faith and, therefore, must be valued and promoted. Such authentic expressions of popular piety are not at odds with the centrality of the Sacred Liturgy. Rather, in promoting the faith of the people, who regard popular piety as a natural religious expression, they

predispose the people for the celebration of the Sacred Mysteries.[3]

The correct relationship between these two faith expressions must be honored in that the particular devotion does not supersede or replace the liturgical action. Liturgy is always preeminent. The different forms of popular piety are optional, but not so the liturgy. They each have their specific place in the economy of salvation.[4] In addition, devotions are not considered part of liturgical worship, even if they are performed in a church or led by a priest. This is an important point since the Church studiously guards liturgical practice and worship because Catholic theology is summarized in liturgy.

Popular devotions tend to be on the conservative side while popular movements tend to be on the more progressive side. "Popular piety has to be continually evangelized, so that the faith which it expresses may become more mature and authentic."[5] These pious exercises and devotional practices must be permeated by the following:

- Biblical spirit
- Liturgical spirit
- Ecumenical spirit
- Anthropological spirit

This arrangement should strive to be in dialogue with contemporary sensibilities and imbued with a clear pedagogical awareness if it is to be aligned with the liturgical guidelines of the Second Vatican Council.[6] Within this context then, how did we get to this point in our Church history? In the next two chapters, we explore the slow, historical progression of devotions and how they came into our common understanding and practice of the Catholic faith.

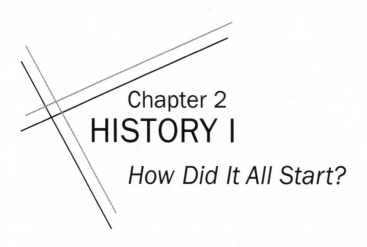

Chapter 2
HISTORY I
How Did It All Start?

Without the study and understanding of history, we are doomed to repeat the mistakes of the past. When we incorporate an insightful reckoning of history, we are amazed by the present unfolding of God's work in our midst.

Devotionalism has a long history in the culture of the Catholic Church. Although traces of it can be found in the early years of Christianity, it was during the Middle Ages that it burst into full flower. The Middle Ages is the period in history between the Classical period and the Renaissance (fifth–fifteenth centuries). We use the word *medieval* to describe the people, places, things, and events of this period.

This devotional mentality was essentially a product of the intense religious fervor brought on by the various reform movements of the Church, the growing laicization of spirituality independent of the monasteries, and the spiritual climate in the cities, where long-established pagan beliefs and practices had become integrated with folk religion. Devotions of all kinds flourished: pilgrimages, veneration of relics, Marian devotions, penitential practices, meditations on the passion of Christ, and more. Richard Kieckhefer, professor of history and literature of religions at Northwestern University, has made a comprehensive study of this period, and I am deeply indebted to him for his insights. The following pages are a close summary of his work in this area and provide us with insights into the historical development of the devotions we know today.

Devotional piety in this period placed a strong emphasis on the humanity of Christ. Four practices stand out in particular: The Rosary, the Stations of the Cross, the Christmas crib, and eucharistic processions. The development of the Rosary was essentially a late medieval phenomenon focusing on meditations on Mary, the life of Christ, and salvation history. The Dominicans enthusiastically encouraged the recitation of the Rosary. The Stations of the Cross centered on the developing devotion to the passion of Christ and the holy places associated with his life. The Christmas crib, derived from a vision experienced by St. Francis of Assisi, expresses a devotion to the incarnation of Christ. Eucharistic devotions, often connected with processions and the Feast of Corpus Christi, also grew in popularity. The image of the Sacred Heart, in literary and artistic form, can be traced to the last centuries before the Reformation began in the sixteenth century.[1]

As literacy increased among lay urban Christians, a notable development occurred: the increase and popularity of devotional manuals. People of all classes enjoyed pious literature such as *The Imitation of Christ* by Thomas à Kempis, *The Golden Legend* by James of Varagine, and myriad other works. Devotional art was expressed in a variety of forms, from ornamental books, to small ivory panels and woodcuts for private devotion, to large polyptychs decorating major altars in churches. The awe-inspiring stained glass windows of the great gothic cathedrals, and later on, magnificent art pieces such as the Pieta and the Madonna of Bruges inspired the masses in a very public forum. "This explosion of devotional forms unmistakably changed the tenor of Christian life."[2]

History I

The rise of devotionalism has been viewed both favorably and unfavorably by theologians and historians. Dutch cultural historian Johan Huizinga (1920–2008) notes the increase in devotions as one key element in the "general diffuseness of late medieval culture." He notes the "extreme saturation of the religious atmosphere"—an ever-expanding menu of benedictions, relics, cults of saints, and so on. In Germany, Protestant theologian and church historian Bernd Moeller saw the desire for such devotions as a sign of "churchliness" in pre-Reformation Germany. Perhaps against all the odds, the faithful, rather than turning away from the ecclesiastical milieu, "hungered insatiably for [the Church's] blessings."[3]

Some embrace devotionalism as their particular form of spirituality, that is, as their core means of connecting with God, while others look at it as a "popular piety" that may do no more than offer feelings of self-contentment. The late medieval lay movements of Franciscans and the Beguine women both demonstrate that devotional themes and practices were often an important backdrop to mystical writings and experiences.[4]

Devotional religion eludes a precise definition because of its diffusive character. However, Kieckhefer locates devotional piety on a conceptual map between liturgical exercises, which are in principle public and official, and contemplative piety, which is fundamentally private, unofficial, and unstructured. Devotional piety stands as an intermediate phenomenon in that smaller or larger groups can practice devotions, but individuals can cultivate them as well.[5]

Devotions are expressed in three main ways: in literary texts, in artistic representations, and in embodied exercises. Literary sources take several different forms of expression:

1. Meditative works (prayers, moral exhortations, reflections on the life of Christ) for individual use

2. Works for public performance (religious drama, pious lyrics sung by a group)
3. Sermons by laity or clergy (preached in a church or outdoors)
4. Collections of sermons, anecdotes or lives of the saints[6]

Devotional art had a tremendous influence on the populace, mainly because people are traditionally inspired and converted more powerfully by images rather than by concepts. Scenes from the life of Christ, the story of the Virgin Mary, and the legends of the saints were favorite motifs, whether expressed in symbolic, iconic, or narrative form.

Devotions historically were primarily a matter of action rather than reflection. Praying, fasting, almsgiving, penitential practices, undertaking pilgrimages, or participating in processions, and other embodied expressions, were common in this medieval period. Unlike liturgical religion, which focused on special times and seasons, devotional practices usually focused on sacred places and objects. Relics, images, and consecrated hosts were the object of devotions. Meditation on the crucifix was the favorite practice for many saints of this period.[7]

The range of devotional motifs in the late Middle Ages was quite extensive, but the four most important were focused on the passion of Christ, Mary, the saints, and the Eucharist.

The passion held a vital but seasonally limited space in liturgy, but it was all pervasive in late medieval piety. Bernard of Clairvaux, Francis of Assisi, and others promoted a spirituality that encouraged meditation on the humanity of Christ. This then led to a focus on the Holy Land, where Jesus lived and died. The obvious connection of the passion with Jerusalem then followed. In the later Middle Ages, the Franciscans served as guardians and guides to the holy places. The standard tour included "stations," or particular places important in the story of Christ's passion. One account in the fifteenth century lists over one hundred of these stations. Pilgrims gained indulgences by praying at these spots or venerating them with kisses and prostrations. Returning pilgrims would often set up replicas of these stations back at home. The crucifix was a common focus of devotions for individuals and for roadside shrines as well. Some authors began writing reflections for individual use as they meditated on these stations. Then in the early sixteenth century, John Pascha, a Belgian Carmelite, created a list of fourteen stations similar to those used in the modern era. These passion-centered devotions give us an example of some of the ways that literature, art, and performance could be linked.[8]

During the late Middle Ages, art became more complex in its depiction of the crucifixion, adding more figures to the scene. Literature on the passion became quite diverse in content and form. In the fifteenth century, interesting detachment from the narrative context developed. This was especially seen in the fondness for particular emblems of the passion: the flagella, the crown of thorns, the veil of Veronica, the instruments of crucifixion, the wounds of Christ, and the wounded heart of Christ.[9]

One of the most significant developments in the late medieval literature of this period was the rise of passion plays, usually performed outdoors by a cast of laypeople. These plays drew their material from liturgical texts, gospel accounts (both canonical and apocryphal), commentaries, and other sources. They creatively developed a whole cast of characters to embellish the story. Devotion to the passion inspired a feverish intensity in late medieval piety.[10]

Kieckhefer points out that "alongside devotion to the passion, and often linked with it, Marian themes were ubiquitous in late medieval Christianity."[11] Relics, shrines, and pilgrimages, feast days, hymns, legends, plays, paintings, statues, devotional treatises, and theology were all present in abundance. There is ample evidence of Mary's humility, but also of Mary's majesty and regal status. Liturgical development in the early Middle Ages produced four Marian feast days: the celebration of the purification, the annunciation, the assumption, and the nativity of Mary. Numbers of other feasts were added as years went on.[12]

Following the example of the Cistercians, the Franciscans helped to disseminate the idea of Mary as universal patroness. As a result, Marian shrines were found everywhere, many of them displaying relics of her hair, vials of her milk, and snippets of her veil.[13]

Artistic representations of Mary during this period represented two primary categories: iconic portrayals of the Madonna (both in painting and in sculpture) and scenes from her life. Scenes from Mary's life were especially common in the panel paintings of the late Middle Ages. These paintings fall into four main groups: those connected with the stories of Mary's childhood, those relating to Christ's infancy, those dealing with Christ's passion, and events that occurred after the canonical Gospels.[14]

Prayers to the Mother of God were numerous. These included but were not limited to the angelic salutation of Luke 1:28, the Ave Maria (Luke 1:42), and the Rosary. The multiplication of these and other prayers served to calm the mind and allow the practitioner to "move into a different space." Marian piety made its way into music as well, as witnessed by the large number of extant motets written in her honor.[15]

Like devotion to the Virgin Mary, the veneration of saints was firmly grounded in liturgical practice. Throughout the early Middle Ages, bishops and synods had control of the canonization process, thus allowing the local communities some say in the naming and choosing of which saintly individuals to honor. However, this all changed around the year 1200, when the pope asserted his sole right to canonize saints. This was no small matter, in that the process then offered a larger cult following of the saint. Once canonized, new saints could then be honored with a full range of liturgical and devotional tributes such as invocation in public prayers and the dedication of churches in their name. Their relics could be encased in precious vessels and displayed for veneration, and they could be represented in art with a full halo.[16]

Whole communities vied for this public approbation because it brought respect, revenue, and pilgrims to their doorstep. The relics of the saints, whether the bones, clothing, or articles that had touched the body of the saint, usually formed the focus of the devotion. Even the smallest item was seen as representing the whole person of the saint. To have touched or venerated the saint was to have shared in the holiness of that particular individual. Pilgrims would often seek special favors through the intercession of the saint. When they received the requested favors, the people would bestow upon the shrine special offerings for the blessing rendered. Some people seeking a specific cure might spend the night beside the tomb of the saint.[17]

In art, the saints could be viewed either in portraits or in narrative scenes from their life. An elaborate system of artistic symbols or attributes helped the observer to identify the saint. Veneration of the saints was also promoted in literature through hagiography collections such as the Dominican Archbishop of Genoa James of Voragine's *Golden Legend*. Affection for the saints can also be seen in the adoption of the saint's names as patrons or baptismal guides. This was the genesis of what we refer to as Christian names. Patronage also was seen in the naming of different ecclesial organizations.[18]

In the late Middle Ages, there developed a fascination with the eucharistic host itself, whether within the liturgy or outside it. This seemed to have originated in the Diocese of Paris, around 1200, with the practice of elevating the host after the consecration. By the middle of the century, the custom had spread throughout Western Christendom. The evolution of this devotion is fascinating in that it was encouraged by the clergy as a means of highlighting the newly promulgated doctrine of transubstantiation. This certainly fed the popular appetite for the miraculous and the "uniqueness" of the symbol. To add to the excitement, bishops were granting indulgences for eucharistic veneration and bells were rung at the moment of elevation. This then became the focus of the whole Mass—to *see* the elevation.[19]

Then this moment was magnified when the host was displayed on the altar outside Mass in a golden vessel called a monstrance. These were often modeled after reliquaries and very ornate in design. The very act of seeing the host, in the fourteenth to fifteenth centuries, was sometimes thought to have a kind of magical effect with the bestowal of special benefits. Another trend that grew out of this paraliturgical devotion was the veneration of the Eucharist in the closed tabernacle. This custom was fostered by the penitential spirituality at the time and the bestowal of indulgences.[20]

With the institution of the eucharistic Feast of Corpus Christi, at the behest of the Belgian visionary Juliana of Cornillon (1192–1258), eucharistic devotion was brought to another level—that of outdoor processions. In northern Europe, these processions began to have a life of their own as the local populace added different amendments to the concept of gathering to honor the eucharistic host. These included but were not limited to the carrying of banners, statues, ornaments, and the ringing of bells. In some places, games and diversions of all sorts added a local secular color to the experience.[21]

Devotion to the Eucharist received strong support from numerous reports of miracles connected to it. These extraordinary miracles were seen, by many, as confirmation of the potency of the Eucharist, but perhaps distracted the faithful from the essential focus of transubstantiation. Shrines were often built at the sites of these miracles. This only added to the popular sense and practice of venerating the Eucharist, but not receiving it. Although prominent philosophical and theological scholars such as Nicholas of Cusa, John Tauler, and Meister Eckhart publicly encouraged reception of the Eucharist rather than extraliturgical display and veneration, popular piety won out. Even the mystical experiences of these respected men could not win them over![22]

Here we acknowledge that the Eucharist was seen more as a focus for devotion rather than as a sacrament. For this reason, the Fourth Lateran Council (1215) saw the necessity of promulgating the decree for annual penance and communion. Nicholas of Cusa, as papal legate to Germany in the mid-fifteenth century, said, "The Eucharist was instituted as food, not as an item of display."[23]

"Taken in their historical setting, these devotions are certainly not to be condemned. If the people of that time had not been given these devotions, they would have had nothing at all and they would have lost all Christianity. Since the liturgy had become inaccessible to them (because it was not in their language), something else had to be substituted for it"[24] that would meet them where they were. Such forms of piety focus on a sentimental kind of religious "experience" in place of the mysticism of the larger Christian tradition.

From this cursory historical overview of devotions in the Middle Ages, we can note the following general trends in devotionalism:

1. The developments that occurred in late medieval piety were cumulative, in that we notice proliferating variations on traditional themes, not new tendencies.

2. The devotions that evolved were lay imitations of monastic practices and other pious exercises.
3. Devotions of all kinds tended to focus on some sort of sacred space, public or private.
4. The intermediate position of devotions, between the public liturgical acts and the private act of contemplation, provided not only flexibility, but also a sense of linkage between church and home.
5. Devotionalism often went hand in hand with particular organizations or communal groupings (a kind of miniature church). Devotions could then become symbolic reinforcement for social or political boundaries within society.
6. Devotions represented a mixture of clerical and lay initiative.[25]

The majority of these devotions became intensely controversial during the sixteenth century. Martin Luther and other like-minded reformers saw devotionalism as unduly focusing on outward public practices. However, devotional fervor continued to persist in the Catholic Church, undergoing further development in the Counter Reformation and through to the modern era. We now turn our attention to that particular era.

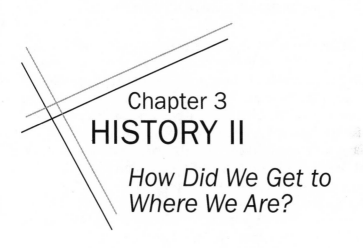

Chapter 3
HISTORY II

How Did We Get to Where We Are?

In this chapter, we trace the ongoing historical developments and meet the significant actors who shaped the devotional milieu we know today. This short history of the development of Catholic spirituality and devotional belief from the late Middle Ages to the twentieth century, draws extensively on the outstanding work of Otto Grundler, director of the Medieval Institute at Western Michigan University. I am indebted to his insights and have closely followed his presentation of this material.

The Middle Ages

The late medieval ages produced a religious reform movement that came to be called *Devotio Moderna*. Under the influence of Geert Groote (1340–84), a highly educated layman of Deventer, it began in the Netherlands and quickly spread into Germany. In 1374, following a conversion experience, Groote left everything and entered a Carthusian monastery where he stayed for three years. Encouraged by the monks, he became a successful itinerant preacher preaching reform and encouraging his listeners to band together in leading a spiritual life. He also created a stir among the clergy when he denounced their worldliness. As a result, his license to preach was revoked. A year later he died of the plague.[1]

By the time of Groote's death, a group of disciples calling themselves the Brethren of the Common Life were living in community in Deventer. A parallel development took place with a group of women who had been living in a house donated by Groote himself. They called themselves the Sisters of the Common Life. By the middle of the fifteenth century, this rapidly expanding movement throughout the Low Countries and Germany counted over a hundred houses. The Sisters were laywomen, while the majority of the men were priests or candidates for the clerical state. Like the Sisters, the Brethren practiced the monastic ideals of poverty, chastity, and obedience, but without taking solemn vows. They followed the daily monastic patterns of Liturgy of the Hours, periods of silence, meditation, and study. Eventually, however, they incurred the wrath of the mendicant orders—primarily the Dominicans and Franciscans—for creating a new monastic order without solemn vows, thus violating the mandate of the Fourth Lateran Council in 1215. Shortly before his death, Groote foresaw this issue arising, and so encouraged his followers to found a monastery at Windesheim (present-day Netherlands). Other monasteries joined to form the Windesheim Congregation, which, by 1480, eventually numbered eighty monasteries.[2]

Groote believed that authentic spiritualty necessitated the correlation between interior devotion and external works of piety. This was seen as viewing the way to God as a life of struggle, of contempt for the world, and of self-denial. This included a denigration of academic learning, which became an enduring characteristic of *Devotio Moderna*. The key focus is on imitation of the person of Christ, through a fusion of the subject and the object, the knower and the known. One of the prime tools for this work is the daily practice of *lectio divina*. Thomas à Kempis, canon of Mount St. Agnes, in Zwolle, Netherlands, built upon the writings of Groote and other spiritual predecessors in summarizing medieval spirituality in his classic book *De Imitatione Christi*. Christ is the model of self-knowledge, self-mortification, humility, and obedience. He sees this as the way of the cross for all believers. The key word is *imitatio*, an internal imitation of appropriate attitudes, emotions, and self-awareness, and an external imitation of acts and gestures. The *Devotio Moderna* was dedicated to the reaffirmation, renewal, and conscious practice of connecting the interior life of the believer to the person of Christ, and to stemming the tide of spiritual deterioration and lax discipline.[3]

The Modern Era

The nineteenth and twentieth centuries saw the emergence of many new and diverse forms of Catholic spirituality. A detailed study of these movements is beyond the scope of this book. We can, however, survey certain common characteristics and representative figures for this period. David Tracy, distinguished professor at the University of Chicago, offers us a brilliant summary of these two hundred years.

Arguably, the two most influential nineteenth-century figures in the study of Catholic spirituality are John Henry Cardinal Newman and Baron Friedrich von Hügel. Newman's insistence on doctrine as a grounding principle for all revealed truth was balanced by an equal emphasis on personal experience. For him, faith was a deeply personal assent to revelation, which led him to declare that conscience must never be violated. Newman, however, insisted that the individual conscience is formed within the community of the Church, through its teachings and disciplines.[4]

Tracy, summing up the position of this saintly and erudite intellectual, declares that

> doctrine, sacrament, tradition, community, and, above all, church as Body of Christ comprising three equally indispensable functions form the spirituality of Catholics in all cultures. This formation allows a great diversity of spiritual paths while uniting them in the central reality of the Spirit's indwelling presence to the individual soul in communion with church as the spiritual presence of Christ.[5]

This spiritual sense greatly influenced the major decrees of the Second Vatican Council.

Von Hügel's work may be seen as a development of Newman's insight into Catholic spiritual diversity-in-unity. Through the lens of philosophy, he broadened this insight to include the reality of religion, as well as the Church. Von Hügel believed that "analogous to the emotional, intellectual, and volitional elements in the person, religion exercises three principal functions. It continuously needs to develop each element and its interrelationships to the other elements to achieve the balance and harmony of an authentic personality."[6] Both of these thinkers insisted "on the constant spiritual need for Catholics to critically discern corrections and developments of these three functions as well as the contributions and promise of modernity for Catholic self-understanding."[7]

Every theology and philosophy gives birth to a particular spirituality, as evidenced by the number of orthodox spiritualities in Church history (e.g., Thomas Aquinas and his Dominican spirituality, Bonaventure and his Franciscan spirituality, and Anselm of Canterbury and his Benedictine spirituality). The modern period produced several different streams of Catholic theologies and philosophies. Briefly, here are a few of the devotional paths that evolved over the years.

The German Jesuit Karl Rahner, the most influential theologian of the twentieth century, developed and deepened a "transcendental" theology that was profoundly incarnational in its expression. He joined both kataphatic (God is...) and apophatic (God is not...) elements in this spirituality, emphasizing that Christian spirituality is to be found not only in the extraordinary experiences, but also in the most ordinary of human actions (sitting, eating, serving) as reflections of God's reality in our midst. His sense and reference of mystery elevated these actions to a different awareness that could touch every human being. For this reason, he actively encouraged the exploration of other routes of theology such as the mystico-political, liberation, and world centric.[8]

Bernard Lonergan, the great Canadian Jesuit theologian, sought to mediate the meaning and value of religion for a culture. His ability to translate theological language into accessible form for the average person conveyed his conviction that love must precede knowledge. "Religious conversion provides the human being with a new horizon and thereby a new orientation that profoundly affects all knowledge and action."[9] He centered spirituality and theology on the reality of God's love. Lonergan's work (open to historical consciousness and science) was "rooted in the Catholic sense of the need for unity-amid-increasing-diversity. By his argument for the needed shift from classical to historical consciousness, Lonergan showed theology a way to welcome that diversity" while remaining faithful to the larger tradition.[10]

Pierre Teilhard de Chardin, the gifted French Jesuit scientist, theologian, and philosopher brings a different vision to traditional Catholic spirituality. Through the poetic lens, he offers us a new way of looking at the incarnation as a deep affirmation of matter and earth. This then leads him to reinterpret the Cosmic Christ of the Pauline and Johannine biblical traditions through an evolutionary perspective, thus opening up the view of the cosmos as an unfolding diaphanous sacramental gift of God's mysterious immanence. This in turn brings us back to the mystical element in a new and modern form. Teilhard believed that Christians should acknowledge and experience their innate communion with God through creation. All the theological lessons are hidden in nature for us to reflect on. "All creation drives toward new differentiations, greater complexity, and ever greater convergence of ever-new unity-in-differentiation." Understood spiritually, this movement is "the drive from matter to spirit to person to Christ."[11] Teilhard's spirituality firmly rests in the creation and incarnation, and specifically in the physical resurrection of Christ. It is both otherworldly and this-worldly; a spiritualty that affirms both spirit and matter, cosmos and earth; a creation spirituality that is focused on love as the central essence of the Creator, ourselves, and the cosmos.[12]

Hans Urs von Balthasar, the Swiss theologian, has a negative view of modernity, and so seeks to recover the kataphatic tradition for a greater incarnational sensibility. He emphasizes the role of beauty as the shining forth of truth in the visible form, Christ being the highest form. He returns Catholic spirituality to a firmer, more traditional terrain; the sacramental sense of the importance of ritual, drama, icon, image, symbol, and word itself. In looking at the saints, for example, we see God's love in visible form; it is images that inform and transform human beings much more profoundly than concepts. For this reason, von Balthasar sees the cross as an essential expression of this truth. His theology gives equal credence to the sufferings, conflicts, and tragedies of human existence alongside the joy of creation and resurrection.[13]

The beginnings of the mystico-prophetic movement in the twentieth century seem to have emerged with the Trappist monk Thomas Merton. His prolific writings sought to bring the rich varieties of the mystical tradition into contemporary terms. He had a knack for drawing often-conflicting Catholic spiritualities into plausible spiritual options for contemporary life. His own writing style elicited a common connection with the readership that garnered him countless followers. Like many of his readers, Merton was a man at peace, and yet not at peace, as he struggled to discover a bridge between the rich Catholic tradition and the ever-shifting contours of the contemporary world. He was looking for a spirituality that was both authentically Catholic and plausibly modern.[14]

This search led him to the tradition of darkness found in Catholic mysticism and the apophatic elements in the writings of many people of a similar persuasion. Later, he also studied the concept of emptiness (sunyata) in Zen thought and Tibetan Buddhism. Merton was a man who became a true bridge between Eastern and Western thought in the field of contemporary spirituality. He asserted that every human being is an image of God's own self, and that despite the devastating effects of a distorted individualism, there is an invitation to recover our "true self." He learned to embrace paradox—to live in the world and yet not be of the world. His apophatic spirituality led him to engage in dialogues with Zen Buddhism. At about the same time, Merton committed himself to a mystico-prophetic spirituality of action for peace and justice. This rare combination of interests opened up a truly radical Catholic spirituality to a world church of ecumenicity, and to a prophetic ministry of nonviolence that is open to the wisdom of other spiritual traditions. Merton's work continues to speak to the spiritual yearnings of this age.[15]

Dorothy Day, a writer, social justice advocate, and spiritual leader, believed that life in the Spirit could only be lived in community. Insisting on the dignity of every human being as members of the family of God, she held that life in community did not mean a withdrawal from the socioeconomic reality of the world. On the contrary, Day developed a Catholic spirituality wherein the prophetic call to social justice must be understood as at the heart of the Christian spiritual life. Through her conversion process, she came to believe that "all is grace" and that love in action was the central way to bring the reality of God to life. This active, participative spirituality was greatly influenced by the Russian authors Dostoevsky and Berdyaev, as well as the French cofounder of the Catholic Worker movement, Peter Maurin. Day and Maurin approached this theme of communitarian Christian personalism on two fronts: the intellectual, through their advocacy newspaper, the *Catholic Worker*; and the active, through the founding of numerous Houses of Hospitality for the poor. Their unfulfilled dream was to have a House in every Catholic parish in North America. Day, like many of her contemporary social activists, recognized the rootless, spirit-bereft character of the modern world and believed that a new saintliness was called for. This immersive sanctity would be a new kind of mystic-prophetic spirituality that actively worked for justice and peace. Living a life of voluntary poverty, she reminded us that we belong to each other and are responsible for each other. Her legacy and impact continue in the twenty-first century.[16]

The Second Vatican Council theologically affirmed a new worldview—post-Eurocentric and global. Since then, a series of new Catholic spiritualities have emerged around the world. David Tracy points to a new paradigm shift toward a mystico-prophetic model with different forms, expressed variously, for example, through developments such as the following:

1. Liberation theologies that focus on justice
2. New creation-centered spiritualities with their recovery of nature and the cosmos

3. Openness to other spiritual traditions through wider ecumenical and interfaith dialogue

It is equally important, in our day, to emphasize the continuing integrity of more traditional forms of Catholic spiritualities. As might be expected, certain pious practices from the past have declined in popularity; nevertheless, in many places throughout the world, Marian piety continues to garner a large following (e.g., Lourdes, Fatima, Medjugorje, Guadalupe, and Czestochowa).[17]

At the same time, the classical traditions of Catholic spirituality still thrive in ever new and varied forms. Add to this the development of new religious orders and secular institutes, and we see that the original Spirit finds new means to live in the modern world. Three figures stand out as key representatives of the *caritas* tradition: Thérèse of Lisieux, the cloistered Carmelite, Charles de Foucauld, the hermit-priest who lived among the Tuareg of Algeria, and Mother Teresa of Calcutta. Each in their own way helped to articulate new ways to actualize *caritas* in the modern setting.[18]

Thérèse, through her life and autobiography, offered the "little way" as a simple means to practice *caritas* in everyday life. Charles and Mother Teresa offered new ways of living the *caritas* tradition amid the poor and marginalized. Both expressed in specific acts of love for the poor, the outcast, and the dying the concrete power of transformative love. Both founded or inspired religious communities to continue their original visions.[19]

Healthy spirituality is always grounded in the context of the present period of time and its unique particularities. Thus the emergence, in the twenty-first century, of developing and challenging spiritualities; some inspired by the biblical revival, some by the Second Vatican Council's call to involvement in social and political justice, and others by papal social encyclicals, and the emergence of political theologies in Europe. Such inspiration was spurred on by the rapidly increasing growth of vast numbers of poor persons and impoverishing situations throughout the world. The practitioners of these forms of spirituality see the struggle for justice for all persons as the heart of the Christian understanding of complete transformation in Christ. This is forging a new unbreakable link between the power of love and the struggle for full justice (personal, economic, cultural, political, and religious).[20]

In theological terms, the founding document for this "preferential option for the poor" is the work of Peruvian theologian Gustavo Gutierrez, *A Theology of Liberation* (Orbis, 2015). His writings have influenced liberation theologies and spiritualities in Asia, Africa, Europe, and the Americas. These theologies offer a hermeneutic of suspicion regarding the roles of women at every level of the Church. This new complex sense of biblical-prophetic justice will probably generate a thorough rereading of Catholic institutional, intellectual, and religious life inspired by the feminist retrieval of "forgotten" spiritual resources and prophetic feminist suspicion of injustice to women.[21]

The prophetic call for justice has also helped Catholics to broaden their understanding and praxis in areas such as the ecological crisis and the threat of a nuclear holocaust, perceiving such outreach as an avenue of protecting life in all its forms. Thus, the call to creation-centered spiritualities has led to a study and reincorporation of some neglected aspects of Catholic spirituality: the wisdom traditions of the Scriptures, the Franciscan tradition with its vision of right relationships with all creatures, and the nature-oriented traditions of Africa and the Americas with their emphasis on the cosmos and a greater respect for our embodied nature in relationship to all of creation. Part of this search will inevitably involve a larger opening of Catholic spirituality to the other religious traditions.

Most recently, we have seen this interest continuing through Pope Francis's encyclical *Laudato Si'*.[22]

The Second Vatican Council, aligned with the various revivals of the study of Scripture, liturgy, and patristics have encouraged a greater ecumenical attitude and interreligious dialogue. This opportunity has opened the way for a more pronounced sharing of different theologies, spiritualities, and mystical experiences from various cultural perspectives. This exciting work has unlocked the need for a mystico-prophetic option for our times that encourages the hope for a global and dialogical spirituality. Central to this hope will be "the firm foundations" laid by Newman and von Hügel for the "three elements" of Catholic Christianity (the institutional, intellectual, and mystical).[23] These will be sure guides and reliable theological underpinnings in the ongoing development and evolution of Catholic popular piety.[24]

With this historical background in mind, we now turn our attention to the four primary areas of devotional focus: The saints, Mary of Nazareth, the Eucharist, and the passion of Christ.

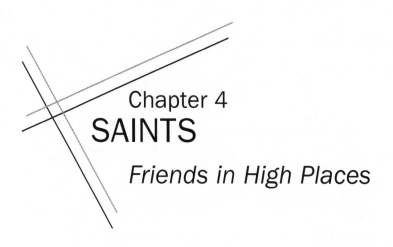

Chapter 4
SAINTS
Friends in High Places

I am a priest of the Archdiocese of Los Angeles, and we are privileged to have, in our cathedral of Our Lady of the Angels, a magnificent and heart-stopping visual of the company of saints. A series of contemporary tapestries by artist John Nava forms a kind of dual processional along the side walls of the nave, showing over 130 saints of every historical period, all facing the altar, literally with their eyes on Christ. Every time I find myself in the cathedral, whether on a quiet, personal visit for reflective prayer, or as a liturgical concelebrant, as I walk up that center aisle, my heart is flooded with the realization that I am never alone on my journey. I am accompanied by a vast array of fellow travelers who have shared my faith, my struggles, and my strivings. I wonder if there is any other place in the world, including all the great cathedrals and shrines, where the company of saints is more powerfully depicted. I have not found one.

Saints come in a wide variety of flavors, colors, and personalities—young, old, women, men, famous, and not so famous—bringing with them a vast array of rich and fascinating life stories. We tend to be drawn, psychologists tell us, to those who hold for us some rejected or undeveloped part of our own sanctity and integrity. Perhaps this is God's way of inviting us into the deeper waters of holiness and aligning us with a guide to accompany us on our journey.

The biblical conception of the holy people of God is fundamentally egalitarian. From the earliest days, all members of the Christian community were acknowledged as saints, participating in the holiness of God through the paschal mystery of Christ. In the ensuing centuries, the age of martyrs added further companions of hope, offering encouragement and inspiration in dangerous times. The subsequent inculturation of the Church within the Roman system of patronage led to a fundamental shift in the people's understanding of saints. Until the third century, the saints had mainly been seen as witnesses in a partnership of hope. This all changed between the third and fifth centuries, when they began to be viewed as primarily intercessors and patrons in a structure of power and neediness.[1]

The interplay of the companionship and patronage models formed an accommodating relationship to the veneration of saints. However, the later developments of the liturgical celebration of All Saints' Day, and the use of the term "Communion of Saints" in the Apostles' Creed encoded the companionship model into official teaching. Invocation of the saints, linked with the idea of patronage, can still find renewed meaning when practiced within a community of equal disciples in grace, linked across the world and beyond death.[2] "The ultimate object of veneration of the saints is the glory of God and the sanctification of man [sic] by conforming one's life fully to the divine will and by imitating the virtue of those who were preeminent disciples of the Lord."[3]

Historically, the veneration of saints has taken many different forms. Since the early centuries of the Church, relics and images have been an important means of connecting with the memory of a saint, both individually and communally (e.g., reliquaries, tapestries, statues, and stained glass windows). Miracles were often credited to the placement of, or holding of, particular relics. This motivated many towns and villages to lay claim to the bodies of saints in order to gain economic benefits from the pilgrims visiting the burial sites or former living quarters of the saint. This often led to great conflicts between towns or city-states. Unfortunately, this unedifying spectacle continues to some extent to this day.

The feast days of saints were always an important time for people to pause from their normal routine of work, and to celebrate with Eucharist and festivities, which often included processions, plays, and a good deal of food and merriment. At one point during the late Middle Ages, these saints' days (both local and universal) accounted for approximately two thirds of the calendar year.

The prayers to saints often took the form of a novena (from the Latin *novem*) requesting special graces or answers to particular intentions. This is an ancient tradition of praying, in private or public, for nine successive days or weeks. The custom stretches back to the apostles' mandate to wait in prayer for the coming of the Holy Spirit after the ascension. Saints are seen by many Catholics as intercessors, intervening for us to God for our own needs. These prayers have often become standardized and shared with the community.

An important means of connecting with the saints and their power of influence has always been through pilgrimages. This embodied custom, developed in the fourth century, has continued to grow and expand to the present day. At its heart, a pilgrimage is the process of traveling to the site of a holy person's residence or final resting place, seeking a favor (healing, forgiveness, reconciliation, miracle, conversion, etc.). This often involves physical challenges like fasting, walking numerous miles in a single day, sleeping less, and experiencing limited comfort, in addition to penitential practices. For pilgrims, this is seen as a heroic type of prayer—encountering God in several different ways—through nature, fellow pilgrims, in silence, loneliness, and physical limitations. A few years ago, my friend Fr. Patrick Mullen and I embarked on a pilgrimage from Porto, Portugal, to Santiago de Compostela in Northern Spain. For all the above reasons, it was a transformative experience for me. I was surprised at how the experience felt as though it was embedded within me and remained with me for a very long time. I can understand why so many pilgrims regularly pray this way.

Most of us are familiar with many of the canonized saints, especially the universally known ones like Francis of Assisi, Ignatius of Loyola, Teresa of Avila, Catherine of Siena, and so on. Our knowledge of saints has often been limited to our own cultural purview; however, there are over ten thousand canonized saints mentioned in the Roman martyrology. Many of these saints are better known in their local regions, cultures, and countries. Does this mean that these are the only ones "in heaven"? No! Canonization simply means that the Church officially recognizes that, by their exemplary life on earth, these people have been received into eternal glory. In an extensive ecclesial process, an examination of their lives and often their writings has determined the authenticity of their sanctity. One thing that the Church looks for in those being examined is whether and how they integrated their contemplative life with their actions. This social concern aspect is especially important for us Christians; Jesus was very clear that love of God is intimately connected to loving service of others (Matt 25:31–46). Faith and beautiful spiritual practices are useless unless they are connected to regular acts of service (Jas 2:14–19).

How are you being invited by Jesus to translate your piety into social action?

The main reason that we have a disproportionate number of clergy and religious in this category of canonized saints is that the ecclesial process requires a great deal of assiduous and detailed work on the part of numerous skilled individuals (and religious orders) who have the time, interest, and money to undertake the necessary research work. There are countless numbers of sanctified people in heaven, enjoying their eternal reward, who will never be brought to the attention of the Vatican authorities.

St. Augustine was fond of saying, "There are many people that God has that the Church does not, and many that the Church has and God does not." Remember that quote when you are feeling discouraged in your own spiritual growth. God has you in a beautiful embrace of merciful love that extends into eternity.

Feminist theologians, notably Sr. Elizabeth Johnson, CSJ, distinguished professor emerita of theology at Fordham University, in her remarkable book *Friends of God and Prophets: A Feminist Theological Reading of the Communion of Saints*, have tirelessly pointed out the disappointing lack of "official" feminine voices in the Church contributing to the field of hagiography. Johnson delineates five ways that a different feminine viewing of the lives of holy women can reinvigorate our appreciation of their contribution to our faith history:

1. Rectifying distorted stories in Scripture and tradition (e.g., Hagar and Mary Magdalene)
2. Reassessing the values of the virgin martyrs (i.e., self-definition and empowerment)
3. Reclaiming the silent, anonymous voices of women throughout history
4. Narrative memory in solidarity (so healing can take place)

5. Subversive memory (written, spoken, named, witnessed)[4]

Reading the lives of the saints as autobiographies or biographies has been a very traditional practice for encouraging us on our own journeys of faith. When I was a boy, I loved to read comic books about heroes overcoming deadly enemies or reconciling an impossible situation. Little did I realize that this practice was preparing me for reading the lives of the religious heroes and heroines called saints. This is something that I have done regularly for many years and helps me to keep the eyes of my heart focused on the Lord and not on me. Recently, I have also been reading the lives of holy men and women outside the confines of the Catholic faith. I have found this to be richly rewarding as well.

Who are your heroes and heroines? What are the predominant themes that you have discovered in their lives?

Saints are often extolled for their particular brand of piety, their ascetical practices, or even their eccentricities. They can, and perhaps should be, models for us in general, but not necessarily in particular. Ascetical practices, separated from the context of one's life or chosen out of a misplaced zeal, can be damaging to one's person (e.g., self-flagellation and extreme deprivation of food, water, and/or sleep). Healthy asceticism flows out of a life of prayer and discernment. God does not need these particular practices; rather, we do, to help us move beyond our egocentricity in particular.

What disciplined practices help you in deepening your relationship with Jesus?

Saints

To put things into perspective, I would like to mention a few aspects of the Church's approach to sanctity in general and saints in particular. Holiness is not about multiplication of devotions or prayers. These religious elements are possible ways to holiness, but they are not signs of holiness. They can point us in the direction of God, but they can also become a source of self-idolatry. Rather, holiness involves growth in inner freedom, virtue, and right relationship with all people.

Are your prayer forms helping you to become transformed?

Holiness is not something that happens instantaneously; rather, it is a lifelong, gradual process that is nurtured and developed in discipline and focus. The particular discipline is unique to each saint. The common denominator is a clear focus on Christ, which is confirmed by an exemplary life of virtue. Each saint is imperfect in his or her own way, but they all have notable virtues that flow from their relationship with Jesus. Their unique personality comes to wholeness or fruition in the vibrancy of that relationship. No one would confuse the saints in terms of their identity, because the grace of God works effectively with the particular reality of each individual within the context of their life.

What are some virtues that are growing in your life of prayer and holiness?

People do not become holy all by themselves; they need the assistance of faith companions and the faith community. For this reason, many saints had spiritual friendships with other like-minded individuals. Think, for example, of Francis and Clare of Assisi, Teresa of Avila and John of the Cross, Francis de Sales and Jane de Chantal. They assisted and encouraged each other, sometimes through their presence, often through letters. Furthermore, following the way of wisdom, saints often had spiritual directors or wise guides to steer them in the right direction (Prov 12:15).

Who helps accompany you or guide you on your journey of faith?

I think it is important to acknowledge that many saints regularly practiced private devotions that grounded them in their faith. This became a "formal foundation" for their mystical experiences. Their individual theologies and experiences were well within the larger Catholic framework of spirituality. While every saint is unique, there is a similar energy about these holy people—an energy that flows from the same Creator. It seems that each has had an individual experience that shapes their awareness of God and moves them to loving service of others. The devotionalism of Teresa of Calcutta moved her to reach out to the poor and dying, affirming their dignity in God's eyes. Vincent de Paul, through his devotional practices, was directed to compassionate care of the poor and outcasts as well as the reformation of the clergy.

What particular devotions ground you in the awareness of God's love and open you up to all other people?

Saints are friends of God who intercede for us and walk with us on the journey of holiness. We venerate them but we do not adore them. This respect or reverence comes from our own relationship with Christ, who reminds us that we belong to each other; we are all part of God's forever family called the Communion of Saints. We can learn from one another and create our own spirituality, guided by the example of others. This is how the different schools of Catholic spiritualities developed throughout the centuries—through sharing, practicing, and learning from each other's mistakes.

Which saint helps you to grow in your own journey of holiness? Is there anything you have in common with any of these saints?

Another way of connecting with the saints is to remember that they are on the journey with us. We can imagine them walking with us as companions of hope, encouraging us and affirming us. Their writings and prayers can sustain us when times get bleak or lonely. We can ask for their intercession. We can also choose a beautiful likeness of them (a holy card, framed painting, or picture) to put in a special place where we can see it often. Medals are worn for the same reason. These images are mirrors of our inner life. They are reflections of our own inner figures, energies, and unconscious yearnings to be acknowledged and integrated into our conscious life. For example, the desire to be a person of prayer or wisdom, or to be of service to a great cause.

Elizabeth Johnson's interpretation of the Communion of Saints is composed of these five elements:

1. The community of living, ordinary persons as "all saints," in particular as this designation is used to characterize members of the Christian community

2. Their working out of holiness through creative fidelity in ordinary time

3. Their relation to the circle of companions who have run the race before who are now embraced in the life of God and accessed through memory and hope

4. The paradigmatic figures among them
5. The relation of this community, living and dead,
   to the whole community of the natural world[5]

Taken together, these five elements offer us a contemporary systematic symbol that is open to many intellectual and practical consequences.

Johnson offers us a way of letting the symbol of the Communion of Saints sing again. She reminds us that acts of remembrance and hope serve to reawaken within us the ancient perspective of companionship and friendship. One way this can be done is through prayers of praise and thanks to God for the witness of the saints and the prayers of lament for their destruction. This sets up a relationship of mutuality. The petitions are not explicit but implied, as in any intimate relationship. Another way to resurrect this attitude of collaboration is by celebrating All Saints' Day with a different perspective. This is the day in which we celebrate the unknown holy ones of God, the ones whose lives made a difference, victims of injustice, individuals we have known and those alive today, filled with God's grace. A third way is through creating new litanies that name the realities of our society and open our hearts to new ways of relating. Other examples include, but are not limited to the following:

- Stained glass windows with contemporary saints
- Contemporary icons and sculptures
- Newly crafted lives of the saints of all faiths, races, and nationalities
- Calendars of holy people

Having said all this, how can the saints inspire us? How can they have a deeper meaning for us? How do they model for us? And perhaps most importantly, is there a real-life connection between these holy women and men and us who are living as we do, in a world immensely distanced in time and space from most of them?

Jesuit priest Jim Martin's classic book *My Life with the Saints* provides an extraordinary and yet very personal exploration of these profoundly important questions. His language of "meeting" and "coming to know" the saints immediately takes us to a new place in our veneration and devotion, and invites us into their presence with us, so that we are no longer viewers and supplicants, but intimates of these great, but often very ordinary, figures.

Fr. Martin begins his journey not with the miracles, the asceticism, or the spectacular religious practices of some of these women and men; rather, he begins where he himself is situated. He begins in the ordinariness and sometimes messiness of American life. His discovery of some of his favorite saints comes from his love of cinema, the reading of a book, inspiring relationships, French lessons, a television show, as well as the predictable sources of Scripture, images, and frescoes.

Who would have thought?

With disarming honesty, he brings to the discussion his own life—his attitudes, his beliefs, his hopes and dreams, his prejudices, his disappointments, his experiences, his relationships. And in this reality, he discovers saints whose journeys in various ways paralleled his own.

Why is this approach so powerful? Because the greatness, the holiness, and the inspiration of the saints are rooted in their very humanity. In the way they dealt with the ordinary humdrum, or even the dramas, of their lives. They had an unshakeable trust in God's will for them, in God's intimate involvement in their lives, and in God's all-embracing love calling them beyond themselves in every situation, every challenge, and even every failure. For me, one of the most inspiring aspects of the Nava tapestries at the cathedral of Our Lady of the Angels is not just the egalitarian composition—no saint is larger, more highlighted, or hierarchically positioned above any other—but the presence among them of several unnamed figures, who remind us that we, too, belong in that procession, and a place is reserved for us.

The saints share our humanity, our struggles, our triumphs, our longings, and our vulnerability. They lived, as we do, in a particular setting of time and place. The twentieth-century American Trappist monk Thomas Merton has made perhaps the most powerful observation on this subject: "For me to be a saint means to be myself." Indeed, that is what this community of holy people, canonized or anonymous, wants for us: the wisdom that they discovered in their own lives. That wisdom is the legacy that they bequeath to us today.

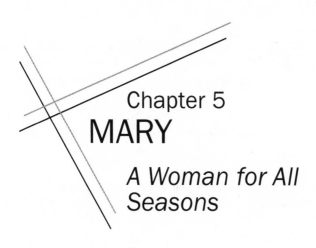

Chapter 5
MARY

A Woman for All Seasons

How do we approach a reflection on the most enduringly honored and beloved woman ever to grace this earth? Beyond fame, beyond celebrity, beyond universal popularity, she stands as the most powerful symbol of all that is good, true, and faithful in womanhood—indeed, in humanity itself— pointing us always to the center, to her son Jesus. To him she gave her life, in him she discovered God's plan for her, with him she suffered, and beside him she invites us, in ways beyond counting, to experience the same full journey to salvation.

Every culture and every era has interpreted Miriam of Nazareth differently. Pope Paul VI in the apostolic exhortation *Marialis Cultus* (Marian Devotion) made clear that our understanding of the Virgin Mary must always be understood in relation to Jesus and should include a solid underpinning of biblical, theological, liturgical, ecumenical, and anthropological principles:

> When the Church considers the long history of Marian devotion, she rejoices at the element of cult it

shows, but she does not bind herself to any particular expression of an individual cultural epoch, or to the particular anthropological ideas underlying such expressions. The Church understands that certain outward religious expressions, while perfectly valid in themselves, may be less suitable to men and women of different ages and cultures.[1]

This has not, however, been the basis of the average Catholic's understanding of Mary and her role in the Church. Ideally, such an approach would mean that God would be at the center of any devotion to Mary, and that she would be clearly presented and placed in relationship to Christ and the Church. This is why the conciliar documentation about the Virgin Mary in the documents of Vatican II is placed in chapter 8 of *Lumen Gentium* (the section about the Church) and not in a separate document.[2] She is one of us.

My introduction to Mary was as a child through the prayers of the Church, principally the Rosary, litanies, and novenas. This led me to view Mary as above me, even beyond me. I had nothing on which to ground my experience except the encouragement of others. This approach continued until my seminary studies. I knew that I needed a more rational contribution that could assist me in my adult life and relationship to Mary as companion on the journey.

How were you first introduced to the Virgin Mary?

We have little historical knowledge about Mary. We know that she was a first-century Palestinian Jewish woman, with Semitic features and Mediterranean coloring of skin, hair, and eyes. She, like the Jewish women of her time, would have "occupied the lower rung of the social and economic ladder, and her life was lived out in an economically poor, politically oppressed, Jewish peasant culture marked by exploitation and publicly violent events."[3]

There are only about a dozen specific scriptural references to her. In the Gospels, Mark's view of her and her role is not overly positive, while Matthew's view is somewhat more neutral (e.g., Joseph, rather than Mary, is highlighted in the birth narrative). Luke portrays her positively as a woman of faith who participated in the early Christian community in Jerusalem, while John offers the reader a more stylized version of her role.[4] These views cannot be easily harmonized. "Pious exercises cannot remain indifferent to the results of biblical and theological research on the Mother of our Savior."[5]

What aspect of Mary's life in Scripture propels you beyond passive devotion?

Mary walked by faith and pondered on things in her heart. She was a partner with God in a great unexpected adventure. Her patriarchal marriage is superseded by God's plan to collaborate with an impoverished peasant woman. For this reason, she becomes our sister, our mother in the faith, modeling for all of us how to be a disciple of Christ. Like Mary, we are to hear the Word of God and put it into practice. We remember Mary as friend and prophet to inspire our own witness and to encourage the poor and oppressed.

Her model is to become our own way of discipleship in doing the will of God. The scriptural account of Mary's annunciation has five structural aspects that are common in annunciation stories throughout the Bible:

1. An angelic being formally greets Mary.
2. The message is delivered.
3. Mary responds with doubt and an objection.

4. The angel reassures her.
5. She ponders the message and agrees to the invitation.

In this particular annunciation, however, the language is that of a new creation, rather than a miracle. Mary fully participated in this astonishing co-creative work. This is important. Mary models for us how to hear and interpret the Word of God for our own time. Jesus affirms this prophetic role (farsightedness) much more than he does her biological participation in his life (Luke 11:28). Therefore, to follow Mary's example we are to do the following:

1. Hear God's Word.
2. Hold it in our heart and ponder it.
3. Put it into practice.[6]

How does this incarnational process take place? Mary is the model. She joins in her own person the material and the spiritual reality, just as Jesus will do in his life. It happens by the gift of grace and through surrender and choice. This means an unconditional yes to our destiny and a commitment to live it in such a way that it benefits the larger global community, not just our own individual plans.[7]

How do you follow Mary's example of hearing God's Word to you?

Until the fourth century, there were no notable Marian devotional practices. Marian devotion really flowered after the Council of Ephesus, when Mary was declared *Theotokos* (Mother of God). This public declaration of Mary's role in the story of humankind's redemption awakened in the Christian community a desire to honor her in specific ways. From the fourth century onward, various devotions developed around Mary, including the following:

- Proliferation of icons, statues, and other artistic expressions
- Medals and scapulars
- Titles, roles, and symbolic expressions
- Rosary
- Novenas
- Angelus and antiphons
- Litanies
- Crowning of Mary as Queen of Heaven
- Solemnities, feasts, and memorials
- Apparitions

Which of these pious practices have been a part of your own faith life?

Much has been written about the abundance of religious trappings around Marian devotion. However, apparitions are another matter; they are difficult to explain. They are private revelations, usually reported as visual manifestations of Mary, sometimes a series of related appearances over a period of time. These apparitions are thought of as maternal expressions of Mary's care for the Church. Normally the purpose of these visions is to draw attention to some aspect of the Christian life or message within a particular context. Mary appears to people, not to bring heaven to them, but rather to expose the heavenly dynamic within them. Sometimes people have reported supernatural phenomena accompanying the apparitions. There are usually strong similarities among the visions. The recipients are often poor and unschooled children. Obviously, there is a strong psychological connection between these experiences and the individual's inner life. Since the third century, there have been over eighty thousand Marian apparitions reported by individuals. The Church has authenticated only seven (e.g., Our Lady of Lourdes and Our Lady of Guadalupe). This does not mean that the other revelations have no value, only that they are *private* revelations that may sustain the individual in their own faith journey. These revelations do not have the *public* approbation of the Church. Clearly, real discernment is needed here.

Four solemnities of Mary are related to Marian doctrine, ranked in order of importance. This shows the gradual historical and theological development of our understanding of Mary's participation in the work of salvation:

1. January 1: Mary, Mother of God (*Theotokos*, or God-bearer). The Council of Ephesus (431). Honors Mary as Mother or caregiver/nurturer.
2. March 25: Annunciation (new creation/virginal conception of Jesus). The Council of Constantinople (381). Focuses attention on Mary as Virgin being autonomous, independent, and living from the center with integrity and wholehearted engagement.
3. December 8: Immaculate Conception of Mary (Mary is truly redeemed as she is graced before her response). Pius X (1854). Mary as companion or friend.
4. August 15: Assumption of Mary (Mary is who we shall be). Pius XII (1950). Mary symbolized as a wise woman.

What we say about Mary we should be able to say about ourselves as followers of Jesus. Beauty, mercy, faithfulness, generosity, and the other attributes of the scriptural Mary are to be incarnated in us, not simply honored in her. Officially speaking, the Church does not worship Mary. Rather, she is a symbol for the Church itself, as is evidenced by the Vatican II documents on the Church. However, on a popular level, the Virgin Mary is more than venerated. As Queen of Heaven, she is, for all intents and purposes, worshiped. Popular devotion will almost invariably win out over liturgical rubrics and theological guidelines, and it has always been so.

During a sabbatical in 2013, I had the opportunity to visit many of the Catholic sites in Chile and Argentina. I remember one church in particular in Santiago. Santo Domingo is a Dominican church built in 1747 that highlights the Virgin Mary through the sheer size and placement of her statue atop the tabernacle in the sanctuary. She is the dominating image viewed from the body of the church. The lighting and staging say it all: this is the most important aspect of this church. The much smaller statue of Christ in the sanctuary is hidden from view by the large presence of Mary's statue. There is much to ponder in this display of devotion.

Which experiences of Mary or popular devotions have led you to deeper reflections on your own humanity?

In studying Marian iconography and titles, scholars have found several similarities between the Mary cult and some ancient goddesses of various cultures. As a Church, we often chose pagan feast days (e.g., December 25 was the Roman feast day of Saturnalia in honor of the sun deity Mithras) and sacralized them. Likewise, we often chose pagan sites of worship (e.g., Chartres cathedral in France was built on an ancient Druidic sacred site) or veneration for our own churches. This should not surprise us. It is a fact that when pagans converted to Christianity, they often substituted Mary in place of a goddess known by a particular title or image (e.g., the early

Coptic Christians and the Egyptian cult of Isis and Horus).[8] Such a historical understanding should not upset us, because it lets us know that this metaphor speaks to a mystery that is larger and vaster than any of our words or images can ever be. Alternatively, to put it theologically, God uses ordinary reality to express the extraordinary mystery of the Godhead.

So, what is going on here? We might look to depth psychology for some answers. It is accepted that the unconscious is energetically charged with ancient preexisting patterns called archetypes that are stirred to conscious expression by any encounter with historical realities that corresponds to their meaning. Archetypes are universal themes that are cross-cultural, trans-historical, and trans-religious, which are often expressed through images. "Mary, because of her historical content, awakens nearly all of the luminous archetypes of the feminine that lie hidden within our interior archaeology."[9] The great Marian mysteries constitute special points of emergence and interaction for many unconscious images.

Archetypally speaking, then, Mary carries the energetic symbol of mother (maternal), virgin (interdependent), companion (friend), and mediatrix (wise woman) in her cultic following. These are the four principle aspects of Marian doctrine in the Catholic Church. These doctrines are meant to nourish us on our own road to individuation or wholeness. As Mary embodied these particular archetypes in her own life, we are to do likewise.

Contact with Mary feels numinous to us, as psychoanalyst Marie-Louise Von Franz says: "Whenever we contact the deeper archetypal reality of the psyche, it permeates us with a feeling of being in touch with the infinite."[10] Over time, the focus of the Mary cult (or religious devotion) has unfortunately shifted from a symbolic, metaphorical celebration of these mystical truths to a more literal and dry interpretation that lends itself to superstition rather than transformation.

Mary

Mythical images, symbols, and metaphors are larger than life in that they tap into the archetypal imagination. They can serve a transformative function by recreating or repairing our fragmented wholeness. We fragment when we lose touch with our spiritual identity.[11]

How do you bring together material and spiritual reality in your own life?

The Mary cult will continue to flourish wherever it is encouraged by religious or political authorities, or in areas where patriarchy still rules as an anthropological phenomenon.[12] This devotion is unconsciously supported by the popular acceptance of the overreaching masculine imagery for God.[13] Think of the magnitude of devotion in Latino cultures to Mother Mary. This is primarily based on the culture and anthropological reality of a strong patriarchal system. We can also look at the strong matriarchal connection with Mary in the Filipino culture.

Mary has been presented as the ideal feminine (passive, obedient, meek, humble, forbearing, patient). There is no eternal or essential feminine. We are all created equal in God's eyes. Mary reveals her own unique nature through the glimpses that we have of her in the Scriptures. For example, in her Magnificat, she proclaims a God who enters human history to reverse the order of power and powerlessness. In the visitation, Mary sets out to visit her cousin, Elizabeth with courage, determination, and spirit.[14]

Over time, Mary accumulated virtues and titles that once belonged expressly to God (e.g., mercy, compassion, and tenderness). This development was compensation for the aforementioned strict patriarchal image of God. It would be much better to allow the motherly, maternal imagery and terms that we use for Mary to return to God where they belong. This will help us enrich our vocabulary and understanding of God as well as honor Mary more authentically.[15]

How is your image of God evolving over time?

In the late Roman Empire, patronage was an important social construct. Patronage was a practice whereby an individual would seek out a person occupying a high place of prestige or power, hoping to induce that person to intercede for them in matters of finance, career advancement, or general social benefits. This patron/client relationship is not found in the New Testament era or the early Church; it was a model belonging to the secular world. A better image to lean into is the metaphor of "a cloud of witnesses" or friends and companions on the journey cheering us on.[16] The saints can do this because they have been where we are now. In this way, we become partners in hope. The memory of Mary should be as a friend or companion on the journey. She is the archetype of what a complete Christian should be. As such, the more we isolate Mary from Jesus, the less tangible and credible we make her.

So, to take Mary off her pedestal, we need to

- Understand her as a member of the Communion of Saints
- Remember her as a first-century Jewish peasant woman
- Refuse to see her as the maternal face of God, the eternal ideal of the feminine, or the perfect woman[17]

How might this internal work change your image and understanding of Mary in the Church?

If we do this necessary work of removing Mary from the pedestal, then an authentic Marian spirituality would include the following:

- Reflecting and owning the annunciations in our own lives (Luke 1:26–38)
- Praying the Magnificat as a means of pointing us onward along the journey (Luke 1:46–55)
- Practicing fidelity in times of trauma, loss, and despair (John 19:25–27)
- Linking the story of our life to the Scriptures and the larger Tradition (Luke 2:21–24)
- Embracing our full humanity, even the dark, painful, unknown, and mysterious aspects (Luke 2:25–40, 41–52; Matt 12:46–50; Mark 3:20–22)
- Integrating a contemplative approach to life (Luke 2:19, 51)
- Practicing the gift of compassionate presence and kindness (John 2:1–12; Luke 1:39–45, 56)
- Pondering prayerfully the will of God leading us to action (Luke 1:26–38)
- Participating in the work of the Church (Acts 1:14–15; 2:1–4, 14–21)[18]

Today, as a lifelong Catholic, I approach Mary as an adult with my questions, struggles, and requests, creating my own adaptations and prayers that come from the depths of my being. Probably the most traditional Catholic form of address to Mary—certainly in terms of requests for intercession, but also as a recitation of titles of honor—is the litany.

Litanies, ever a mainstay of devotional prayer, are universal prayer forms that are meant to generate images in the minds of devotees. These images have a dual purpose in that they are helpful in our praise, petitions, veneration, and worship of God or any of the saints, including Mary. Yet they are also meant to act as a mirror to generate descriptions of our own divine potential. For we are motivated and inspired more by particular images than by concepts or ideas. This is the gift of a devotional perspective.[19]

Many years ago, I was introduced to a contemporary Litany of Mary of Nazareth that serves me well in my devotion to Mary. I share it with you as an example of integrating the above reflections in a prayer form.

This litany is true to all that we know of her from Scripture and Tradition, acknowledging her vision (see the Magnificat), her life experience, her fidelity to God's invitation for the entire course of her life, and her invitation to us to take her hand as we make the journey that echoes hers.

The Litany of Mary of Nazareth[20]

MARY,

Wellspring of peace   **All: Be our guide.**

Model of strength

Model of trust

Model of gentleness

Model of courage

Model of patience

Mary

Model of risk

Model of openness

Model of perseverance

MARY,
Mother of the liberator   **All: Pray for us.**

Mother of the homeless

Mother of the dying

Mother of the nonviolent

Widowed mother

Unwed mother

Mother of the political prisoner

Mother of an executed criminal

MARY,
Oppressed woman   **All: Lead us to life.**

Liberator of the oppressed

Marginalized woman

Comforter of the afflicted

Cause of our joy

Sign of contradiction

Breaker of bondage

Political refugee

Continued

Seeker of sanctuary

First disciple

Sharer in Christ's ministry

Participant in Christ's passion

Seeker of God's will

Witness to Christ's resurrection

MARY,

Woman of mercy   **All: Empower us.**

Woman of faith

Woman of contemplation

Woman of vision

Woman of wisdom and understanding

Woman of grace and truth

Woman, pregnant with hope

Woman, centered in God   **All: Hail Mary....**

As with all devotional practices, and prayers, the question here is not "Will she answer my prayer?" or "Can I please Mary with this prayer of praise?" but "How many of these honorifics can I claim in my own living out of my call to becoming fully human and alive in Christ?"

Am I a wellspring of peace?
Am I a model of gentleness and trust and courage?

Mary

Do I seek to liberate the poor and oppressed,
 refugees, and others in bondage?
Is my life marked by mercy, grace, and truth?
Am I, like Mary, centered in God?

If we can begin to answer some of these questions in the affirmative, however fragile and stumbling our efforts, then we are following the call of Mary in her Magnificat, and we can then be sure that we are honoring this woman, the loved and venerated Mother, who forever and always points us to her Son and sets us on the path to true discipleship.

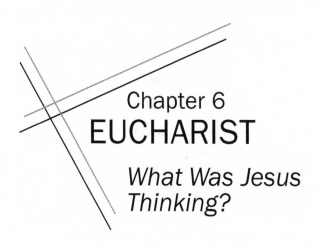

Chapter 6
EUCHARIST

What Was Jesus Thinking?

With this historical review as a foundation, we will now explore the distinction between a more passive devotional approach to the Eucharist and an active approach that is more transformative. This is usually termed a eucharistic spirituality. The celebration and reception of the Eucharist is unique for each person. For some it is a felt sense, for others, an experience of the sacred presence, and for yet others it may be a symbol of Divine closeness. *Is this happening for you?* There are stages of appreciation of the mystery of this event. It is as simple as discovering the extraordinary in the ordinary, and yet as difficult as explaining God.

So, who is God for you? This may seem like a very basic question, and it is; however, it is a necessary question if we are going to unpack the mystery of the Eucharist. God is not so much a person as a life force, an energetic connection, an intimate presence. Jesus gave us the Eucharist to invite us into this energetic presence—to have a genuine connection with the Divine as he did. In John's Gospel (6:53), Jesus makes his invitation very explicit and intimate, as he talks about eating and drinking this presence. Herein lies our nourishment for the journey of life. It is both a promise and a fulfillment of the Divine closeness. This is what we Catholics mean by the Real Presence of Christ in the Eucharist. It is more than a sign; it is much more about the intimate reality of experiencing the authentic manifestation and nearness of God as food for the journey. We are deliberately taking Christ more deeply into our very being-ness. This action is meant to remind us of our already given closeness to God as God's beloved daughters and sons. Surrendering to the mystery and accepting the gift is our work to do. Jesus said it more directly: "Do this in memory of me." "Eucharistic devotion...must integrate two basic principles: the Eucharist is before all else the celebration of the Paschal mystery...[and] all forms of Eucharistic devotion must have an intrinsic reference to the Eucharistic Sacrifice, or dispose the faithful for its celebration."[1]

All of the sacraments flow into and out of the Eucharist, meaning that all of the encounters with God (cleansing, blessing, forgiving, nourishing, healing, unifying, serving, etc.) are extensions of this life-giving force that we call love. Sometimes we are actively engaged with these events, other times these events might act upon us in our passive state. There is a saying by St. Basil in the fourth century: annunciations are many; incarnations are few. Ideally, we come to gradually understand the mystery that we are celebrating and consuming, so that eventually we can embody this mystery for others. *How does this happen for you?*

Catholicism is a "both/and" religion, in that we willingly hold the tension of the opposites (e.g., the Eucharist is both a sacrifice and a meal, we are a holy people as well as sinners in process, Jesus is both human and divine, the Eucharist is both Word and Sacrament). This understanding enables us to enter the mystery of Christ and our own life more deeply. We enter with humility and courage by noticing, savoring, and pondering the events of our lives, as well as the life of Christ. This is similar to engaging in a *lectio* (a meditative process) on our life.

What insights from your own life have you gleaned that continue to nourish you and strengthen you, especially in difficult times?

Daily celebration of the Eucharist did not enter into our regular liturgical practice until the fifth century. Eucharistic devotion, as we know it today, burst into full flower in the late Middle Ages. The focus was much more on oracular veneration rather than active sacramental participation in the mystery. This frequently resulted in a passive response on the part of the laity, to such a degree that most folks stopped receiving the host and instead put the emphasis on *seeing the host*. This concentration on the transcendence of Christ in the host, without any grounding in a healthy intellectual understanding of the mystery, led to much superstition and focus on peripheral matters, rather than the central mystery of transformation.

It is essential to remember that Jesus never invited anyone to worship him; rather, he invited people to follow him. When he said, "Do this in memory of me," he was talking much more about living a eucharistic life, rather than celebrating the eucharistic meal. Therefore, Christianity is an active response to God's love, not a passive reception of the eucharistic species.

There are different ways of looking at or "seeing" the Eucharist:

- The first level is the **literal level**. This involves *observing* the Eucharist as a sacrificial meal, which it is, and much more. It is Christ offering himself to us as nourishment for our journey of faith. Many people stop here and think that this is all there is. This stage is all about comfort. For example, putting the emphasis on how beautiful the music is, or how profound or touching the homily is or how magnificent the church building looks. This is fine as far as it goes, but there is no deeper conversion or transformation.

- The second level is the **symbolic level**. This is the level of *making the connection* between the personal and the communal, the bigger picture with my smaller story. This stage is about entering the Christian story of salvation and ritually honoring my own need for liberation in the present experience of liturgy. *What do I need to do to make salvation real for me?* This is most clearly seen through the expression and active use of meaningful symbols and gestures.

- The third level is the **mystical level**. This is the level of celebrating "holy communion" with the Godhead, *knowing and experiencing* our own divine nature in the fullness of God's immanent Spirit. The experience is unique to each person as we feel "fully embraced by Divine love," as St. Catherine of Siena says. It is being immersed in this intercommunion—a place beyond words. This experience offers a new perspective on seeing/knowing that everything belongs, that reality is singular, relatable. The mystics describe it as a "transformative encounter."

Jesus invites us to follow him (John 1:35–50) through these stages to "see even greater things." *Why stop at the first stage?* He wants us to follow him in ever greater intimacy, ever deepening maturity. He asks us to *fully participate* in this mystery. You might think of it as the difference between putting your toes in the ocean and swimming with the current or scuba diving in the depths of the great ocean. What a tremendous difference between these three experiences of the water of life! The most common word that mystics use to describe this movement with God is *floating.* We are floating in the expansiveness of this energetic love, without any need for fear or worry of any kind, because we are God's beloved.

Theologically, the pearls of Jesus's teaching are hidden in plain sight as we celebrate the Eucharist. Liturgist Fr. Richard Albarano offers a beautiful summary of this theology through a question-and-answer format. Consider this a template for our eucharistic gatherings:

> *What does the eucharistic assembly share in common?*
> - One Lord
> - One faith
> - One baptism
>
> *Why do they assemble?*
> - To serve God
> - To serve one another
> - To serve others
>
> *In what does this result?*
> - Celebration
>
> *How do they celebrate?*
> - Through the Word
> - Through the Sacrament
>
> *What is the result?*
> - A eucharistic community

What are its characteristics?
- A welcoming attitude for others
- A remembering of the mysteries and their significance

With this perspective in mind, what might a contemporary eucharistic veneration or devotion look like?

Sitting quietly before the eucharistic presence in the tabernacle or adoring the Lord during exposition of the Eucharist, you may find it useful to use one of the following practices to deepen your encounter with Christ. Your choices will depend, of course, on your personality and life situation:

1. *Lectio divina* focusing on one of the eucharistic passages in Scripture, especially the Gospel of John
2. Spiritual reading focusing on the themes of the Eucharist
3. Meditation on specific aspects of the eucharistic mysteries
4. Jesus prayer
5. Contemplative prayer
6. Centering prayer
7. Silent words of praise and gratitude
8. Sitting in silence taking in the mystery of the present moment
9. Making regular visits to the tabernacle
10. Creating a eucharistic novena

I also find the following questions are helpful to stimulate some meaningful reflection and meditation:

Eucharist

How do I experience Jesus loving me or nourishing me?
What is the meaning of the Eucharist for me?
Where is God inviting me to let go and receive God's
love more fully?
What is God asking me to let go of in my life?
How is Jesus asking me to be nourishment for others?
What does silence bring up for me?
What scares me about giving my life more fully to
Jesus?
Which part of my life story is Jesus asking to heal?
What do I need to do?
How can I be a blessing for others?
Who or what do I need to forgive?
What really feeds or nourishes my soul? Am I doing
this regularly?

This type of veneration or devotion is meant to move us in a heartfelt way to an embodied response. Sometime ago, I came across a story that illustrates this concept quite clearly.

Ed Casey is the CFO of a well-known firm in Massachusetts. Every morning, whether it is sunny or snowing, Ed makes his way to a local church for some quiet prayer during eucharistic exposition. Believing in this Christ presence opens Ed's eyes to see Jesus throughout the day. He does more than just honor this presence within the ordinary people that he encounters throughout the day. Ed embodies this awareness through an overly generous tip to the server, food and money to the discouraged poor, flowers and visits to the sick, running errands and spending time with the lonely elderly. You get the picture. He becomes a Real Presence (Eucharist) to others. It is prayer and works of service together that proclaim the Christian faith most clearly.

The eucharistic service is comprised of two main parts: The Word and the Sacrament. The brilliance of Jesus as a Wisdom teacher is evident in the choice that he made in creating this experience. He joined two of the most basic aspects of people's lives: story and ritual.

Stories have the power to change our reality. Hence, Jesus told many stories, called *parables*, to liberate people from their limited perspective of life. In traditional societies, the telling and retelling of stories is a sacred activity. It makes it happen again; it makes possible our sense of community and offers us a sense of our personal identity. The story undergirds our moral values and helps us deal with the mystery of creation. In the liturgy, the key stories that hold our attention are the biblical stories of redemption, healing, forgiveness, acceptance, and new life. The central mythic story of Christianity is about death and rebirth. This theme is retold in many ways.

The ritual enacts the story in a transformative way. Rituals are symbolic encoded gestures with a concise meaningful vocabulary for ordering our lives. The language of the soul is symbolic or metaphorical, which is why we use this method in our worship space. Rituals link body and soul in a deeply heartfelt way. The most significant aspect to a transformative ritual is the willingness and ability to surrender to the experience.[2] Full participation in the Eucharist can be such an experience.

A eucharistic spirituality demands a more active engagement from the believer with the story and the ritual in mind. At its most basic level, this approach is focused on four aspects that apply equally to the Word and to the Sacrament:

> **Taken**: holding the reality of your life as it is, reflecting on your life story and your response to it
>
> **Blessed**: seeing, naming the blessings of your life, and asking God to bless the work of your life; offering it up to God (this is the sacrificial part)
>
> **Broken**: opening up the bits and pieces of your life

to allow God's love to heal and liberate you; surrender to this work of grace

Given: share your life in an embodied way through works of service to others; share your wisdom, your insights with others as a messenger of the good news

---

Which aspect of this spirituality are you most drawn to? Which one do you typically avoid?

This eucharistic encounter offers Catholics the opportunity to meditate upon its mysteries and put them into practice. A more detailed involvement in eucharistic spirituality asks us to notice the *movement or action* of the liturgy. Liturgy is not so much what we do but what God does through us. It helps us to face the paschal mystery of our own lives in Christ. Our life "in Christ" is simply living with the awareness that we are not alone on the journey. Christ is immersed in all the details of our life—praying with us, working with us, loving through us, and so on. The paschal mystery is the life, death, and resurrection of Jesus; it is the pattern of our existence as well, both literally and symbolically, as we rhythmically experience order in life, then disorder, and finally, we hope, a reordering. This enduring process is repeated often, at ever-deepening levels.

What does an authentic eucharistic person look like?

To be an authentic eucharistic person, then, is to live these actions consciously throughout the week. This is why we keep celebrating the Eucharist, to remind us of who we are, and how to live mindfully in the present moment. Hopefully, this awakens us to the great mystery of God's ever-present love!

The underlying sacramental principle is straightforward and clear in the practice of the Catholic faith: that which is true always and everywhere must be noted, honored, and celebrated, somewhere, somehow. If this is correct, then we must notice, ponder, and then put into practice these active truths of the Eucharist. Let me give you an example. If it is true that God blesses us, then we must honor this truth somehow. The most common way is to be a blessing to others in word and deed. *When was the last time you blessed your spouse or child with words of affirmation, mirroring their own innate goodness? When was the last time you did something out of kindness for someone with no expectation of a return favor? When have you sent an encouraging card, text, or email to a person who has forgotten their own dignity?* We never outgrow our need to receive blessings from others.

These actions are for our own individual growth as well as for others. It is in the engagement of this activity that we encounter the risen Lord. In practice, this means that Christ is hidden in the everyday activities of our lives: eating, drinking, working, conversing, gardening, and so on. Obviously, this is moving beyond the historical Jesus to the universal Christ (see Col 1:15–18). Here is a simple layout of the eucharistic activity that we are to live daily:

> Gathering Rite (Conflict Resolution: working toward
> compassionate healing)
>> Gathering
>> Welcoming
>> Forgiving
>> Praising
>> Praying
>
> Word (Love Education: communication and mutual
> respect)
>> Listening
>> Reflecting

Eucharist

Responding
Interceding

Sacrament (Ritual Expression: embodied surrender
     to the mystery)
     Receiving
     Offering up
     Blessing
     Breaking
     Sharing

Missioning Rite (Service: art of accompaniment)
     Sending forth the assembly into the world
     Witnessing to the good news

Let me illustrate this insight with a personal story about Bill, my father, during his dying process. About ten years ago, my father was dying from the effects of pneumonia, a persistent plague of his throughout his life. During the last week of my father's life, I sat with him while he wandered in and out of sleep. I was struck with the idea that now was the time for me to *just be present* to my father as he was—no words, no questions, no activity. The image of sitting before the tabernacle came to mind, and so I did just that. I sat and waited in silence. I was given the revelation that now I was embodying a eucharistic spirituality by listening, reflecting, and interceding for my father.

Whenever you do these actions, either singularly or collectively, you are being a eucharistic person. Each section has as its focal point a unique purpose that is meant to work on the believer in a subconscious manner. It is a formational education of sorts, helping us to face the conflicts of our lives with a practiced compassionate love that is ritually supported by accompanying others on the journey. This is a summary statement of eucharistic spirituality.

In the early Church, there were "home churches"—small ecclesial gatherings in private homes—where the believers lived out this reality with a real awareness of this mystery. Today, there are very few of these communities. Perhaps that is one reason why, for all intents and purposes, we have migrated away from the essence of a eucharistic spirituality.

Let me conclude with a story to flesh out this dense summary statement: A young medical student had to be away from his fiancée for a month while he took his comprehensive exams. It was difficult for him to be separated from his love in a time of stress and need. He was riding on a bus traveling to New Haven, Connecticut, when the bus made a scheduled stop at a shabby roadhouse. He sat down at a counter and found himself seated across from an older woman. Meeting his eye, she said sympathetically, "Honey, you sure look depressed." "I am," he replied, as his eyes filled with tears. She simply asked, "What's wrong, honey?" He proceeded to tell her his story, showing her a picture of his beautiful fiancée. Then she began to relate to him the story of her own happy marriage with her deceased husband and how difficult it was when they had to be separated because of his job. She said, "You're going to have a wonderful marriage. Everything is going to be fine." She then suggested he might feel better if he ate something. She ordered a doughnut and broke it in two and gave it to him. At that moment, her bus departure was announced, and she had to leave. It was only as she disappeared through the door that he recognized the visitation in the breaking of the doughnut.[3] God comes to us in this eucharistic fashion throughout our days and our years. *Do we have the heart to receive the gift in times, places, and encounters where we least expect it? More importantly, do we have the eucharistic heart to be that gift to those placed on our path through life?*

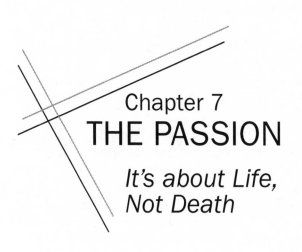

Chapter 7
THE PASSION
*It's about Life,
Not Death*

In the Gospel of Mark, we read, "Jesus went on with his disciples to the villages of Caesarea Philippi; and on the way he asked his disciples, 'Who do people say that I am?' And they answered him, 'John the Baptist; and others, Elijah; and still others, one of the prophets.' He asked them, 'But who do you say that I am?' Peter answered him, 'You are the Messiah.'" (8:27–29). Of all the questions that Jesus asked (more than 300!), this one is perhaps the most important for the contemporary believer: *Who do you say that Jesus is? Who is Jesus for you?* Your answer to these questions will greatly shape your own way of life and your value system.

Yeshua, meaning "Yahweh saves," was born into a pious Jewish family in the hill town of Nazareth in Lower Galilee in approximately 6 BC, a few years before the death of King Herod the Great (4 BC). Jesus, as we know him, grew up speaking Aramaic and would have learned some Hebrew through the biblical readings at the local synagogue. Contrary to the way artists generally portray him, Jesus looked like any other first-century Palestinian Jew: dark-skinned and probably bearded, with short curly hair. Village life was marked by relative poverty, burdened by taxation and high unemployment. He probably became an itinerant carpenter, working in Sepphoris, a large Hellenistic city six miles away, where wealthy aristocratic Jews lived.

After a presumably ordinary and unexceptional upbringing, Jesus was attracted to the movement of John the Baptist, who began his ministry in the Jordan Valley around AD 27 or 28. Baptized by John, Jesus struck out on his own, beginning his public prophetic ministry in early AD 28, when he was about thirty years of age. His activity was focused on his home area of Galilee and Jerusalem (including the surrounding area of Judea). Identifying with the prophetic text of Isaiah 61, and sensing the power of the Holy Spirit in him, Jesus announced the coming of the reign of God. He recognized that people had strayed from God and needed a change of heart. He did wondrous deeds that people understood as miraculous and preached his unique message of the kingdom of God—filled with wisdom sayings, parables, and beatitudes. The end times called for a radical way of life, so he called into question the acceptable ways of doing things, for example:

- Eating only with others in the same class
- Regarding family as the most important relationship
- Rejecting "others," that is, anyone outside one's own tribe, religion, or class
- Holding the law as more important than people or property

His prophetic-symbolic gestures of teaching and healing were ways of waking up his listeners to the more important values of the kingdom of God. He insisted on what we would today call "inclusivity." There were no *others* in God's kingdom.

In AD 30, while Jesus was in Jerusalem for the approaching Feast of Passover, he celebrated a solemn farewell meal, which scholars variously describe as a *Chaburah* (friendship meal) or *Pasch* (Passover memorial) with his inner circle of disciples. He was arrested that night in Gethsemane (April 6, by our modern reckoning) and brought before a group of Jewish officials. They in turn handed Jesus over to Pilate, who condemned him to death by crucifixion outside the walls of Jerusalem. He was around thirty-six years of age.[1]

Why is all this background information so important? Because it grounds us in the reality of who the historical Jesus was, and what he stood for, what he modelled for us. It is from this scriptural witness that we form and interpret our experience of Jesus. As the great fourth-century scripture scholar, St. Jerome, said, "Ignorance of the scriptures is ignorance of Christ."

Huge and important developments in Christology (the study of Christ as the transhistorical, eternal presence of God) happened in the twentieth century, with the advent of the historical, exegetical, and cultural reading of the Scriptures. This expansion of knowledge and understanding worked to counteract the dangers of sentimentality and superficiality in devotion to Jesus. The most life-giving starting point for the study of theology and spirituality is actual human experience, lived in community. Our own life experience in such a setting is the primary word that God speaks to us, as it was for Jesus.

Jesus embodies God's Word. He was God's dynamic presence or "parable." He lived with the same limitations as any other human person. Like us, Jesus gradually formed his human identity through making choices. He had to learn to trust in the dark, to think, pray, ponder, and decide. His experience of God was a first-century Jewish experience during the Second Temple era, within the religious structures of his day. His central and most powerful experience was the "Abba" experience. For Jesus, morality flowed from an inner attitude, or authentic relationship with God. He talked about God metaphorically and in narrative form. He had a unique clarity of understanding and insight. Jesus's fundamental identity was as son of God, although it's probable that he might not have fully comprehended this mystery until the resurrection. He came gradually to this process of self-understanding (Luke 2:52).

There are five different models or theologies of Christ in the New Testament: Mark, Luke, Matthew, John, and Paul. All are correct. These different portraits mean that we can approach the mystery of the historical Jesus through the lens of our own life experience, balanced by the community of faith, called the Church. We tap into Jesus's Abba experience by believing in Jesus's words and life. We must relate our Christology to the cultural world we live in. *Do you not yet understand or comprehend? Are your hearts hardened?* (Mark 8:17).

Jesus dealt directly with people's immediate needs, for he experienced the kingdom of God as already present. It was not just a future promise. "*What do you want me to do for you?*" (Matt 20:32). His work was the manifestation of the presence of the kingdom. He stood always for people first, and considerations of the law or other cultural or religious tenets came after this. Jesus was a special agent in bringing about this kingdom. He incarnated this kingdom through a gradual unfolding process. He offered a healing process that is concerned with the whole person. Jesus modeled a new form of holiness that is grounded in right relationship with everyone, one that leaves the purity code behind.[2]

Jesus came to show us what God is like and what a mature human being can become. He is the personification of the fulfillment of humanity. He reunited God and humanity in himself and in his sacrifice. It was in the depths of his humanity that Jesus discovered his divinity. And so it is for us!

God's plan for Jesus came from his love. The life, death, resurrection, and exaltation of Jesus was the fruit of God's love; it was never punishment accepted by Jesus in place of sinful humanity. In other words, no matter what happened, Jesus kept on loving unto death. His dying process was an active choice empowered by the Spirit. It was his self-less and self-giving acceptance of dying, not his actual death that redeemed us. Our salvation (i.e., our "coming to wholeness") is the continuous active living out of this gift of God's unremitting love. Faith, salvation, and healing are not something that happens to us; rather, this coming to wholeness is a conscious choice and a participative act (see the healing episodes in Jesus's ministry). This is a creative process of transforming human life, individually and collectively, by the power of God. Jesus wants to be a power in our lives—a power to act in his name, to continue his work caring for others. We are now the sacrament of God's presence in the world. Jesus died for our sins in the sense that Jesus permitted God's spirit to re-create through him what we had destroyed by our sins. It is our sins that punish us, not God. God sets us free from over identifying ourselves with those sins and reminds us that our authentic identity is beloved children of God.

Do you believe that I am able to do this? (Matt 9:28)

Without the resurrection, Christianity does not make sense. This is not just a past event. Jesus is risen. Christ is the risen Lord, beyond space and time. Jesus did not come back to life but rather moved into a new life. The Christ experience, having existed from the very beginning, is beyond the historical limitation of Jesus (John 1:1–18; Col 1:15–20; Eph 1:3–14). The word *Christ* describes how God's presence has enchanted all matter. It was a grace-filled encounter of peace, forgiveness, and blessings given to the disciples by the resurrected Lord.

This transforming gift has now been given to us through our baptism.[3]

We are meant to embody this risen Christ, for he has shown us a superior way of being human. God's Spirit is working through the risen Christ in re-creating humanity. The message and the gift are to be shared with the whole world. This great core mystery of Christianity, that God became flesh, continues through the Eucharist and through each of us believers. The unfolding of this incarnation, begun with creation, is now being empowered by the Spirit of the risen Savior. You and I are the very presence of God in the world today. This is what is meant by the Mystical Body of Christ.

So what does this powerful declaration mean? How do we connect with, bind ourselves, and commit ourselves to this great task of transformation of our humanity? We hold, as Catholics, that our primary entrance to this world of "grace" is through the sacraments, celebrated in community. But what about the connection—indeed, immersion—at a more intimate, personal, one-on-one level? This is the space where, over many generations, people have found devotions to be helpful and life-giving in their quest for the embrace of the divine.

There is a plethora of devotions to Jesus and to different aspects of his person as well as his ministry. These devotions that have accrued over time are generally filtered through cultural lenses and artistic expressions (e.g., statuary, icons, holy cards, litanies, and prayer forms). Various cultures have particular devotions to the child Jesus. For example, the Santo Niño de Cebú is widely celebrated in the Philippines. St. Margaret Mary Alacoque (France) developed a popular devotion to the Sacred Heart, which led to the practice of participating in the Eucharist for the Nine First Fridays. "Understood in the light of the Scriptures, the term 'Sacred Heart of Jesus' denotes the entire mystery of Christ, the totality of his being, and his person considered in its most intimate essential."[4] Others have focused on a devotion to the Sacred Wounds of Jesus (St. Mechtilde and St. Gertrude of Helfta) or the Precious Blood of Jesus (connecting us with his passion) or the Name of Jesus (e.g., the Holy Name Society). St. Teresa of Avila had a devotion to the Holy Face of Jesus. Recently, St. Faustina introduced devotion to Jesus under the title of Divine Mercy. Another popular title is the Good Shepherd. Perhaps the most identified sign of devotion in regard to Jesus is his cross. This ubiquitous symbol has great significance as a reminder of our redemption. At this time, the cross can certainly remind us of all the torturing and death mechanisms used to harm people throughout the world.

What are the authentic fruits of these devotions?

While it is certainly understandable that Catholics would be drawn in a heartfelt way to the physical sufferings of Jesus, it is his moral suffering that provides a model for the fulfillment of our own humanity. Theologian Fr. Ronald Rolheiser puts it succinctly: "Jesus gave his life for us through his activity; he gave his death for us through his passivity."[5] Both are theological truths. This means that his dying experience was a lonely process of "letting it be done unto him" as the Father willed it. Jesus modeled for us how to accept the dying process as a transition into the next stage of life.

How does Jesus's passion connect with your passion and dying experiences?

As Christians, we naturally have a devotion to Jesus but rarely to the eternal Christ. The real challenge as followers of Jesus is not to remain admirers of a historical person but to become mature disciples. Jesus never said, "Adore me!" Instead, he said, "Follow me!" While many of the saints had particular devotions and communal venerations as a foundational connection, they recognized that God had bigger plans for them. Their personal mystical experiences were grounded in their works of service and care for the poor and vulnerable. We also are to ground our poignant experiences of Christ in works of compassion and service to the poor and vulnerable.

The real purpose of devotions is to move our hearts to see differently and to act compassionately. This is to become what Pope Francis calls "intentional missionary disciples." Unfortunately, for many Catholics, devotions become habituated and fulfill our yearning for continual comfort, rather than moving us to action. To consciously choose the way of Jesus in our time and circumstance is to be imbued with the Spirit of the eternal, risen Christ. This involves accompanying others in the journey of their life through a commitment to listening, openness, questioning, prayer, awakening, empowering, and equipping.[6] No quick or easy task!

How are you being called or invited to reach out to others?

I invite you to sit in silence and just notice what comes up for you as you reflect on this question. This ongoing invitation from Christ is about reminding us of our connectedness to all of creation, but especially to all people. We belong to each other. The gift of care, service, or ministry for others is a mutually enriching experience that accentuates this truth.

What particular aspect of human suffering are you drawn to as a means of entering your own suffering?

Many people find creative ways to express their suffering: art, music, poetry, body movement, active imagination, Scripture, stories, ritual, nature, therapy, support groups, and journaling, to name a few of these elements. By regularly connecting with one or more of these expressions, you are creating your own spirituality, your own practical ways to express your interior reality.

What are the fruits of your spirituality in relation to Jesus?

Ideally, your spirituality should be positioning you more and more in line with the active values of Jesus's life: compassion, forgiveness, blessing, reconciliation, peace, justice, inclusivity, respect for others, uniting, service, nourishment for others, and/or being a light in the midst of darkness. Historically, every religious founder had his or her own brand of spirituality that attracted others. Invariably this led these individuals to join that particular group in service to others. Who knows, as you share what works for you, others may be drawn to be a part of your contemporary vision of how to live out the Christian message for our own time.

What was Jesus's spirituality?

In studying the Scriptures, we note that his spirituality had these notable qualities:

- **Single-minded focus on the reign of God:** His prophetic message, parables, miracles, healings, simple lifestyle, and martyrdom all affirm this point.
- **Sense of abundance:** Because he experienced his beloved nature and knew Yahweh as "Abba," everywhere he looked he saw expressions of God's generous plan even in the dark and dangerous aspects of life. Hence, his commandments are called Beatitudes: heartfelt ways of being human

and seeing from a place of unity. He was a poet of compassion whose message was love.

- **Kenosis:** His life of love came from his intimate prayer with Abba. He lived to do the will of the Father, emptying himself of any unnecessary distractions. His nonclinging nature allowed him to let things come and go without undue attachment.[7]
- **Transformation:** Jesus slowly became aware that his mission was to all people. His vision was changed by his life experience. He proclaimed a message of forgiveness and reconciliation. This message also moved him to participate in nonviolent ways for justice and peace.
- **New family:** When Jesus left Nazareth to begin his public ministry, he never returned. He never married. Instead, he created a new "family" of followers. This overturning of a key cultural value was instrumental in the way that his community related to each other and to society. This implies an important aspect of his ministry: God wants to transform not only persons, but also cultural structures and institutions that inhibit the full flowering of human beings.

What type of spirituality nourishes you or energizes your faith?

Perhaps the most beloved of all our Catholic devotions is the eight-hundred-year-old tradition of the Stations of the Cross. Designed specifically to help us reflect on the sufferings of Jesus as he proceeded to his death, it is a powerfully evocative recalling of his fidelity to his Father's call to love. But it is only if we have understood and experienced the life of Jesus—

his difficult path of learning, searching, seeking his Father's will, coming to an understanding of the demands of love, and then making choices—that we can fully enter with him into that last walk to the cross and beyond. That is our call, our invitation, and the enduring challenge to our heart, our mind, and our will.

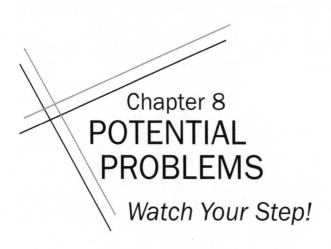

Chapter 8
POTENTIAL PROBLEMS
Watch Your Step!

So, why examine devotionalism at all? After all, devotional practices are a mainstay of Catholic spiritual life. The challenge is that devotions can sometimes devolve into a closed-ended comfort system, which is, in some ways, appealing, but does little to transform us. Because devotions come from the heart, they can suffer all the shortcomings of human relationships. What we need to understand is that they are a means rather than an end in the quest for intimacy, connection, and compassion. We know from our experience of human relationships that these desirable goals will be achieved not through passivity but from activity, and sometimes a combination of both.

My friend Louise grew up in the pre–Vatican II Church, which did not have the benefit of modern theological and psychological developmental tools. In accordance with the Church's recommended practice at the time, she faithfully attended Eucharist on nine consecutive First Fridays and seven consecutive First Saturdays. The promised rewards attached to these practices essentially amounted to a "free pass" into heaven. Louise told me that she did this over and over again to be sure of her salvation. Nowadays, this makes God sound more like a corporate accountant keeping a ledger.

Now where did we go wrong with this sort of approach? Her thinking was incomplete and simplistic, in that she was treating her relationship with God as a contract and not a covenant. A contract is a quid pro quo agreement—I will do this for you if you do that for me. It creates mutual obligation and belongs in the realm of enforceable law, rather than a bond of mutual love. A covenant, somewhat differently, is based on a loving relationship, where trust ensures that the parties will always stand by each other in every situation, including eternal life.

With maturity, Louise realized that the "deal" she had entered into simply did not make sense, and so she began her real collaborative work with God in her journey to salvation. Although she did not deny the value of those devotional practices (they provided her with a solid foundation), she recognized the limits they placed on her own responsibility and on God's active partnership with her. In effect, she had been trying to earn God's love instead of actively cooperating with that already present love.

Devotions are meant to move us, not to move God. The fact is, God loves us already—not because we are good, but because God is good. One of the shortcomings of devotionalism is that it can be driven by pure emotion, with little or no input from the intellect. In a genuine loving relationship, both aspects of our personhood are in play. When the whole person is not honored, making deals becomes the preferred option. We are hoping that if we "do all the right things," then God will be obliged to answer our prayers according to our own prescription. This misconception speaks of a very limited and distorted image of both the God of the Scriptures and the mature human person. At this point, we might raise this question: What about those scriptural promises?

- Ask and you will receive (Matt 7:7a).
- Knock and it will be opened (Matt 7:7c).
- Anything you ask me in my name, I will do (John 14:14).

These are very real promises that Jesus gives us in relationship to the Father. They are not magical enticements; rather, they are relational invitations. When I am in proper union with God, I realize that God's will is generally in harmony with my deepest desires. God, in effect, is partnering with me on my journey, whether or not I realize it. This is the difficult challenge of these Scripture passages. My prayer, then, is entrusting my yearning or desire into God's hands for God is "my rock and my salvation" (Ps 62:2). The reality, as we know, is that not all our prayers are "answered." When this happens, it is not necessarily because of something that we did or did not do. Most times, we will not know the reason for this apparent lack of response.

God cannot be contained, limited, or controlled by any one title, prayer form, or spiritual practice. Ideally, varied prayer forms and spiritual practices open us to the expansiveness of God's presence by creating a greater openness and inner freedom to reality. This is why we need to choose wisely which prayer forms, devotions, and practices will best enable this process. These methods of connecting with the Divine Presence must necessarily be grounded in the Scriptures and Tradition. This is why, in the language of both of these sources, authentic prayer comes from the soil of humility, not control.

There are no tricks, secret Scripture passages, or special prayers that can cajole God into doing what we want (e.g., burying a statue of St. Joseph upside down because you need to sell your house). There is only love between the Creator and us. This is why prayer is about a vulnerability of humbly presenting ourselves before God as we are, not as we want to become. We are to nurture a daily awareness of God and put our trust in the mutuality of that awareness.

When we do not have a healthy understanding of our own humanity or a healthy image of God, we are more prone to misapplications of our faith. For example, I was once called to the home of a Catholic family who wanted me to bless their house because the parents were experiencing marital problems. Now there is nothing wrong with house blessings, or the blessing of cars, buildings, or objects. However, often these requests for blessings are a cover for what people really want: protection from harm, family harmony, financial success, or some vague idea of general well-being. A blessing, rightly understood, is a dedication to God of the person, event, or object. It is the symbolic quest to offer everything to God for God's proper use.

This misunderstanding of God's role, if you like, can lead to some toxic beliefs and practices that can truly harm a person's life of faith. *Toxic* may sound harsh, but in reality, there are certain beliefs that can be—and often are—deadening and destructive in terms of our genuine spiritual growth. Stephen Arterburn and Jack Felton, the authors of *Toxic Faith*, name some of these inaccurate beliefs:

- Material blessings are a sign of spiritual strength.
- I can earn my way to heaven.
- If you have real faith, God will heal you or someone you are praying for.
- Problems in your life result from some particular sin.
- God's love and favor depend upon your behavior.
- Having true faith means waiting for God to help me and doing nothing until he does.
- God is vindictive and waiting to punish me for my sins.

- I must always submit to authority.
- God only uses spiritual giants.
- A strong faith will protect me from problems and pain.

This type of belief system can devolve into a form of "religious addiction" that is often used as a means to avoid reality. Real issues will then remain unaddressed, leading to an infantile approach to life and a greater tendency to blame God when things go awry.

Let's look at a much healthier approach to God and faith. We know three basic truths about God:

1. God loves me more than I love myself.
2. God desires my happiness and well-being.
3. God knows best how I will be happy.

When we start from these premises, we are beginning with the clear and unambiguous proclamation of the good news. So relax and trust God as your ever-present partner in your life. God's will for you is to be authentically alive and whole. Anything that does not do this for you is not of God. This is why the First Letter of John (4:1–3) clearly states: test all spirits. If we do not examine everything, we can easily be led astray from that Voice of love. All healthy spirituality is about awareness, waking up to the presence of the Divine all around us and within us. This process of examination is called discernment.

To create a construct, we might

- Consult Scripture and its precepts
- Listen to the wisdom of trusted others
- Glean insights from personal prayer

- Notice dreams, imagination, and other intuitive sources
- Pay attention to circumstances of life, coincidences, synchronistic events
- Be alert to our own embodied or instinctual sense

It is often helpful to gather information from different sources, weigh possibilities, make judgments, and assess the appropriateness of particular ways forward.

We experience God's guidance through the fruits of the Spirit (Gal 5:22–25) and through our mistakes as well as our successes. When we fail to recognize this solid and balanced approach to the spiritual realm, we can easily be drawn into superstition.

Superstition often lurks at the edge of our consciousness when we turn to devotions and practices that "guarantee" a Divine response. It is an excessively credulous belief in supernatural powers and lack of respect for the natural. Superstitious practices and magic are often in league with each other. Examples of some of these doubtful practices might include the following:

- Wearing particular talismans to ward off evil
- Praying certain prayers nine times a day for nine days to elicit a particular response from God (and if you break the chain, you will be cursed)
- Receiving ashes on Ash Wednesday in the belief that failure to do so will result in you or a family member dying within the year
- Reciting a thousand Hail Marys in the belief that this practice alone will be more potent than one prayer, irrespective of inner disposition

- Excessively repeating particular prayers or devotions, especially in times of fear and anxiety

These types of beliefs and practices only serve to feed a relentless anxiety about a capricious God. The God we worship is revealed in the way we live our lives and in the devotions that we give allegiance. When we neglect to engage our intellect and/or our life experience, the emotions are left to run wild with our perception of the mysterious, the unknown, and the imaginal realm. Faith resides in the imagination, is nurtured by experience, is more deeply understood by the intellect, and is lived out in the activity of our lives. Without this balanced approach, we can unconsciously slip into a variety of dead ends. These are some, though by no means all, of the possibilities:

- Religious addiction
- Scrupulosity (a religious form of obsessive-compulsive thoughts, feelings, or behaviors)
- Pathological self-abuse (excessive penitential practices)
- Blaming all negative experiences on the devil

This is why, in the Catholic tradition, believers are encouraged to seek out a mature spiritual director to guide them on their journey of faith. We can all fool ourselves into believing that what we are doing is right and just, when in reality, we could be walking down a perilous path. My many years of ministerial experience have led me to the conviction that every believer needs, ideally, to actively participate in three arenas of faith life:

1. An ecclesial community that worships together (ordinarily a parish community)

2. A small faith community (where life experience is shared and participants are held accountable)
3. Spiritual direction, mentoring, or an intimate friendship, which mirrors your goodness and helps you to face your blind spots

The most basic and dangerous sin in the Scriptures is idolatry, which is an extreme alienation, love, or reverence for something or someone other than God. With a quick read of the Bible and reflection on humanity in general, we note that we can slip into idolizing anything or anyone when we do not want to face the living God. Believe it or not, devotions can become idolatrous. When a person is unwilling or unable to face or accept their limitations, it is not unusual for them to turn to something over which they can have a measure of control, such as specific prayers or religious activity, repeated at will. Mindless repetition of prayers or practices, no matter how praiseworthy, can impede our spiritual growth. They may be emotionally comforting, but if there is no real spiritual fruit (Gal 5:22–24), then why continue?

I am writing this book in the midst of COVID-19 and the ensuing chaos of great social unrest in America and the rest of the world. I have noticed that many Catholics feel separated from the Church and their local faith communities because the sacraments are not readily available at this time. This "new normal" has spooked numerous good people. Many individuals have sought to fill this void with a multiplicity of extra devotional prayers and practices. More is not necessarily better. It's quality, not quantity, that nurtures our growth in times of disorder and chaos like this. Perhaps a better way to connect with God in this anxious time is to *do less*. To sit in silence or focus on one word or image of comfort (e.g., Jesus, love, or mercy) will do more to help you connect with the deeper realms of yourself and God's ever-present love, than an ever-increasing litany of prayers. It is about bringing an authentic presence to the reality at hand.

Some of us have what might be called a microscopic view of life, which offers the short view, but little breadth, while others turn to a telescopic perspective, metaphorically speaking, that gives them the long view, but gives little depth in return. The first group tends to discover comfort in repetitive routines of prayer forms. These pious prayers can often serve to prevent any further seeking or authentic growth. The second group usually is drawn to spiritual practices that energize their life, but they often forget to connect more deeply or intimately with the Creator.

For many people, devotions seem to be a good replacement for the encounter of God. They are religious, they look good, and others think we are holy for keeping these religious practices. Our dedication and allegiance are admired and applauded without question. What could be so unhelpful about this? Jesus said, "Not everyone who says to me, 'Lord, Lord,' will enter the kingdom of heaven, but only the one who does the will of my Father in Heaven" (Matt 7:21). The *devotions themselves are not wrong*. It often can be our attitude, in that we can use the prayers or practices as a *means* to replace a living, dynamic relationship. It is like a young, engaged woman who might become so infatuated with her engagement ring that she has forgotten the relationship with her fiancé. Devotions are tangible; relationships are interior. Hence, the tension between the two. Devotions are meant to lead us to God, not get in the way of our relationship with God. We are talking about a discipline of encounter here versus a control of reality. A good metaphor might be practicing a "monasticism of the heart" grounded in a real relationship with God.

When we begin with an unreal misconception about the human person and/or the Creator, then we are open to all types of misguided pious practices that usually revolve around controlling our reality. This in turn colors our reading and understanding of Scripture as well as the forms of prayer to which we are attracted. Authentic religious devotions are grounded in our unique humanity with an eye to humbly embracing God's unconditional love for us. As St. Augustine said, what is most important is the disposition of the devotee (not necessarily the devotion itself).

Healthy devotionalism serves as a platform on which we are grounded, so that we can experience the risen Christ. At their best, devotions enrich us by helping us to

- Be present to the moment or reality as it is
- Open up our heart to the overwhelming love of God
- Stay focused on the journey of faith
- Stay awake to God's Spirit and guidance in our life
- Remain on the pathway to ever-deepening awareness of the spiritual life

Any devotion can be an avenue of connection with something greater than we are. Ultimately, devotions are meant to lead us back to the communal liturgy.

What devotion leads you to a place of awe and wonder?

What devotion gives you a deep sense of God's immense love for you and accompanying interest in the details of your life?

Spirituality is the way that we live out our values as disciples of Christ. The practices that we choose sustain us on the journey. The truth is that we walk a broad path that accommodates the cultures, personalities, and the needs of millions of Catholics worldwide. The liturgy, sacraments, and devotions all have their place on this path, and healthy spirituality involves choosing and focusing on what is central to the legacy that Jesus bequeathed to us. To his dying breath, he modeled for us a complete and unerring trust in the will of his Father.

That, and that alone, is our guiding star.

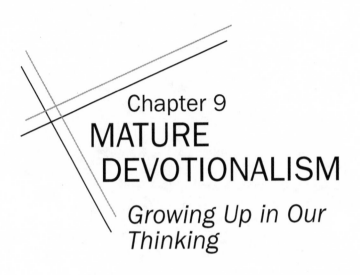

Chapter 9
MATURE DEVOTIONALISM

Growing Up in Our Thinking

As we mature as faith-filled believers, it is imperative that we develop our own spirituality—a spirituality that honors the context, both personal and cultural, of our lives. Otherwise, we will tend to "lean into" old, outdated devotions that may not have any relevance or benefit to our living situation. As we take an honest look at our contemporary setting in this post-modern era, it seems as if we are living in almost apocalyptic times:

- Civil unrest throughout the nation
- A politically divided country over social issues such as civil rights for women, people of color, and differing sexual orientations
- The great and growing chasm between the rich and the poor
- The devastating effects of climate change
- COVID-19 and its aftereffects

- The growing contempt between liberals and conservatives
- The heightened fear and anxiety over the economy
- Increased violence domestically, nationally, and globally

In this type of environment, what would a mature faith look like? Theologian Jane Regan, PhD, of Boston College, offers these perspectives, which I like very much. She says a person with a mature faith does the following:

1. Trusts in God's saving grace and believes firmly in the humanity and divinity of Jesus
2. Experiences a sense of personal well-being, security, and peace
3. Integrates faith and life as a seamless garment, seeing work, family, social relationships, and political choices as part of religious life
4. Seeks spiritual growth through study, reflection, prayer, and discussion with others
5. Seeks to be a part of a community of believers in which people witness to their faith and support and nourish one another
6. Holds life affirming values, including commitment to racial and gender equality, affirmation of cultural and religious diversity, and personal sense of responsibility for the welfare of others
7. Advocates for social and global change to bring about greater social justice and authentic peace for the common good
8. Serves humanity consistently and passionately through acts of love and justice[1]

With a foundation such as this, we can then begin to build a supportive framework of prayer forms and spiritual practices that will reinforce this focus of a mature faith.

What types of prayer do you think will aid you in this important work?

Which spiritual methods will strengthen your commitment to, and focus on, this mature faith?

It is not necessarily an easy or comfortable task, but it is a worthwhile one—and it is certainly achievable. Wisdom teacher Ezra Bayda sums it up this way: "Spiritual practice is a mixture of struggle and integration, of confusion and clarity, of discouragement and aspiration, of feeling failure and going deeper."[2] This difficult, challenging work necessitates an ongoing attitude of patient endurance as we face our individual need for conversion. For many of the saints, devotionalism provided the platform on which they built their own spirituality. In this way, they lived out their value system, one day at a time, slowly surrendering to the grace of conversion. St. Augustine reminds us that there are several layers of conversion that present themselves to us throughout our life:

	TYPE	FROM	TO
1.	Intellectual	Knowledge of facts	Knowledge of meaning
2.	Moral	Satisfaction of law	Values as criteria of choices
3.	Religious	Life as a series of problems	Life as mystery and gift

Continued

4.	Theistic	God is a force	Personal relationship with God
5.	Ecclesial	Church as an institution	Church as a community
6.	Gospel	Concern for my own salvation	Commitment to the kingdom of God

Reality is God's friend. God uses all the details and events of our life as opportunities for growth. Some of these may include the following:

1. An immersion experience: for example, finding ourselves outside our comfort zone
2. Paradoxical situations: experiencing internal conflict when confronted by two or more similar and "good" choices
3. Interaction with creation
4. Intellectual dissonance: conflict between what you have learned and what you have experienced
5. Suffering, loss, and/or death of a loved one
6. Reactions/repulsions
7. Trauma, illness, and accidents
8. Personal issues or stuck points

Part of the conversion process involves our decision to transform some particular attitudes and behaviors that are the antithesis to the Gospel message:

- Every kind of exclusion and elitism
- Sense of entitlement
- Silence in the face of injustice and violence

- Overwork and consumerism
- Disconnection between worship and service
- Judgementalism

Spirituality is not a law to be obeyed but a presence to be seized, undergone, and given flesh to. Once you have taken a long humble look at your image of God and your acceptance of yourself, then you are ready to begin to create a spirituality that will fit the context of your life. What is most important in this work is the disposition of the devotee.

What devotions will sustain you in this extended journey of faith?

Keep in mind that an effective devotion will help open up your heart to God, others, and the world. It sustains you when your heart is broken open by the pain of the world, either in a particular person or event or in the general milieu of living in an imperfect world. Devotional practice will also assist you in being present and awake to the moment so that you do not run away from the place of God's revelation on your pathway to awareness. It grounds and focuses you on the work at hand. Finally, meaningful devotions will benefit you by helping you to experience God's love before you worry about a particular morality.

We Catholics believe we have an obligation and duty to read the signs of the times. It is not an exaggeration to say that this necessary engagement must be grounded in the cultural malaise and religious confusion of the current world situation. Psychologist James Hillman famously said that an illness suffers most until it is correctly named. We live in a time where we have largely lost our connection to the interior life, the place where we most intimately meet God, resulting in an overemphasis on individualism, crass materialism, and a pathological restlessness that hides a deep loneliness. We are trapped in distractions and diversions, concerned with mundane, superficial, trivial, and transient aspects of the external world. We suffer from an illness of the soul that has separated us from the fullness of ourselves and each other, and which has driven us to look for simplistic answers to complex issues. Often this disconnection has led to conflict and violence. Many people continue to look for a particular ecclesial or secular leader to "fix the problem" quickly, without addressing the underlying structures that have encouraged these attitudes to continue. This regression has not happened overnight. Rather, it has been a gradual movement away from a unified holistic approach to our lives.

The solution is right before our eyes, though we often fail to see it clearly, or accept it. It has its basis in Scripture, but also in modern psychology. The process is almost disarmingly simple and consists of four clear steps:

1. Be still.
2. Notice.
3. Ponder.
4. Respond.

Holding the paradoxical tension and ambiguity of a situation without giving into facile, quick responses is a testament to our maturity and our real faith. This is difficult, necessary work if we are to move forward as mature believers. Psychoanalyst C. G. Jung spoke about the need to hold the tension between two choices long enough until a third way or choice emerged. This steady, disciplined work of holding the tension often reveals a much better solution in the long run.

This four-step process of standing still, noticing, pondering, and responding is a faith-filled way of engaging reality, especially when life is confusing. In effect, this is what genuine prayer is. Prayer is not so much about using words but rather, noticing, savoring, and pondering the experience of life. To pray is to be open to the new, the exciting, unfolding mystery of reality. Prayer is the way to life because in prayer we are invited to change and grow in love.

Prayer reminds us to live our lives from the interior outward. Without this attitudinal discipline, we are left wandering in the desert of a world that we cannot control. This is what causes our endless suffering. Prayer reminds us that we have been created in love for love. Anything else is driven by our egocentric desires that are never satisfied. What I am presenting here is an incarnational spirituality grounded in pastoral theology.

Many of us look up to a transcendent God (Creator of the universe) and forget that God is also hidden in our midst as a close presence, holding us in intimacy. We are to hold this Divine expression with reverence and humility, discovering a variety of ways to connect with this life force. For some people, God is experienced in artistic expressions; for example, in a piece of music, poetry, painting, or sculpture. For others, it might be an excursion in nature, intimate relationships, an engaging book, or an experience of wonder and awe.

The spiritual life is about a liberating self-discovery in relation to the Creator and all of creation. Frank Tuoti puts it succinctly: "The spiritual journey is the quest for aliveness and a release from the shackles of mediocrity that deadens the spirit and makes us less than truly human."[3] Our task then is clear: reintegrate the compartmentalized self into a coordinated and simple whole and learn to live as a unified person. No easy feat, which is why we need to remain connected to the Source. "As awareness increases, so too does attraction; as love deepens, consciousness rises."[4]

Sometimes, as we have seen, devotional prayer can be the expression of a subconscious desire to control God. This is the antithesis of real prayer—surrendering to the living God. Then from that place of surrender, we give ourselves to God in service to others, based on our individual gifts and inclinations.

Another danger for many people, who focus only on devotional prayer, is dejection or sadness that is often framed as "God's will" for them. Thomas Merton, who knew something about prayer and about sadness, adamantly names this as sinful:

> There is a sin of sadness. Sometimes instead of trying to react against sadness, we submit passively to it saying, "It is a cross—God wants us to feel that way." No, God does not want us to submit to the sadness that eats the heart out of our virtues and of our interior life. This is a sin. It is a great self-deception to submit to this sadness and feel virtuous over our self-pity.[5]

Remember that religion can be seen metaphorically as the *container* that points us in the direction of God, while spirituality represents the *contents* of that container. The bridge between the two is liturgy. The liturgical sacraments hold in summary form the teachings of the Church, while inviting us into the experience of the Christian mysteries. Spirituality consists of the value system and practices that keep us safely oriented on the pathway of life. It is not an escape mechanism; rather, it is an immersion process. Mysticism is the *felt experience* of the contents. The bridge between spirituality and mysticism is found in devotions. The danger arises when people decide to remain on the bridge and choose not to move forward. This decision inhibits any real transformative work. It is like choosing to remain at a rest stop and forgetting about the destination. God is always calling us forward to the "more" of life.

Contemplative prayer is the normal development of the practice of the Christian life. It is a way of being with the Creator and with all of reality. Often this is manifested in a quiet stance of pure observation, nonjudgmental and open to what is present before us. Silence is an ever-present companion. A contemplative spirituality must saturate all of life, not just one or two periods a day. As Thomas Keating has often pointed out, we must regularly surrender our whole self into the loving arms of God. In this way, we gradually notice an interior transformation of heart and mind (Rom 12:1-2). "What matters is not what one feels but what really takes place beyond the level of feeling or experience."[6]

Most of us, growing up, experienced an emphasis on morality first, instead of on mysticism. This kind of misdirection usually leads to a rule-oriented faith practice based on fear and guilt, rather than a relational belief system grounded in liberation. This early negative experience of religion will rarely support an authentic life-long journey of faith in the midst of conflict or complex issues. Either we will likely tend to remain childish and naïve in our approach to God and reality, or we will walk away from religious practice altogether.

All devotions, sacramentals, icons, and religious celebrations are meant to point us in the direction of God. They act as supports and encourage us on the journey to experience Jesus more often so that we can proclaim him more authentically. They are not meant to be an end in themselves.

A healthy spirituality is grounded in ongoing contemplative or mystical experiences of prayer. For this reason, it is essential that from time to time, in adult life, we must take a closer look at our devotions, and discern whether they are serving to enhance our Christian commitment to personal transformation and social action. Our own Christian faith is always twofold: private and public. The private aspect is nurtured by prayer and spiritual practices; the public expression is strengthened through social works of mercy and justice (Jas 2:14–26).

Authentic Christian prayer forms are embodied in their expression. For example, we are to pray for our secular leaders, but then we put this prayer into action by living our lives with love of, and commitment to our country through different means (e.g., voting, appropriate action for the marginalized and impoverished, care for public places, care for the environment, picking up litter, etc.). This is also relevant when we pray for the homeless and hungry. Our prayer is meant to lead us to actively live out that petition by feeding the hungry and finding a way to assist the homeless.

What prayers for others do you find yourself repeating often?

God wants to answer those prayers through you, since it is God who has put that intention into your heart to pray. Sometimes the best prayer is the one that you feel most strongly about. Imagine it as already being answered.

At the heart of our Catholic faith is the understanding that we are a "both/and" religion. We worship God *and* serve God through, with, and for one another, since we all share in being members of God's forever family. We are to be contemplative and active.

The virtuous life is fed and nourished by a vibrant prayer and devotional life, as witnessed by all the saints. Prudence, temperance, justice, courage, faith, hope, and love do not fall out of the sky just because we desire them. Rather God invites us to collaborate with the Holy Spirit to integrate these virtues into our life. I suggest that you choose a saint where some connection can be made between your own life situation and theirs—struggles, dreams, ambitions, and goals. The saints do not have to be contemporary, but need to be compatible with your hopes, your dreams—indeed, your desired approach to life. In this way, you can hold them up as a model for your own growth and encouragement.

What connects your faith with your intellect, your heart, your body, and/ or your soul?

Theologians, authors, and poets construct words upon words to express ultimate mystery and things holy, in order to connect us with both the intellect and the religious imagination. Artists and musicians create music, paintings, mosaics, stained glass windows, and statuary to touch the heart. First Nation peoples have traditionally created dances, ceremonies, and rituals to be conveyed through the body. People in general tell stories, and choose particular symbols, as a means to soulfully articulate their faith and spirituality. Some find that entering the world of books is transformative for them.

It will come as no surprise that I say this again: when we are dealing with devotions and spiritual practices, quantity is not necessarily better than quality. Christianity is about less rather than more. As Fr. Richard Rohr likes to say, it is not about a "spiritual capitalism" of adding on more prayers or practices. Rather it is about a spirituality of subtraction— letting go of that which prevents us from standing naked before God. Sometimes all it takes is one prayer, one image, or one act of kindness to open us up to the grandeur or magnificence of God. Although this may be a rare occurrence, nevertheless, when it does happen, it leaves us in awe of what God can do with so little.

God has placed the desire for holiness into our hearts to encourage us to seek that quality through prayer, study, and learning from other inspiring role models. Through patient endurance and perseverance, we gradually grow in holiness.

A vibrant spirituality is living, growing, and evolving with the individual person and the community. It is not static!

What prayer forms and practices can help you in this endeavor?

"We are not here to pray our way out of life's challenges. We are here to grow through every one of them into spiritual adulthood. With God at our side, and on our mind, and in our heart, our own spiritual strength and insight grow to full stature."[7] It is especially important to honor our own unique personality in creating an appropriate spirituality. This is about respecting the context of our personal life and the reality that we live in the twenty-first century. Who do I want to become? Ideally, our spirituality should be practical, embodied, and holistic, if it is to align with the Christian ideals. We need to shape our spirituality to reflect, support, and enhance our activity. One size does not fit all. The religious practices are not to be an end in themselves. Rather, they are meant to point us in the direction and consciousness of God.

What I am proposing here is a "second conversion" like St. Peter had after his denial of Christ. Remember that Peter was a good and devout man, like many of the saints. Nevertheless, he needed to go deeper into the mystery of Christ. As Merton has said, "It is relatively easy to convert the sinner, but the good are often completely unconvertible simply because they do not see the need for conversion."[8] As long as this complacent attitude persists, Christianity will stay mired in a certain, limiting malaise. "So far as our spiritual life consists of thoughts, desires, actions, devotions, and projects of our exterior self, it participates in the non-being and exterior falsity of that exterior self."[9] St. John of the Cross, echoing St. Paul, points out that we are to become a totally new person in Christ. This is much more than a conversion from bad habits to good habits. This is the work of grace in conjunction with a heart open to change.

How, then, might we rethink some of our most-loved devotions, so that they

- reflect the reality of our lives, both personal and communal,
- more closely embody the values and priorities expressed by Jesus, and
- lead us beyond ourselves to embrace the needs of the world?

In the world we now live in, it seems a good idea to explore some fresh ideas of how to recreate older devotions in a more energetic and engaging manner for our time and place, as well as looking at some new possibilities. In the final chapter, I offer some concrete suggestions that will help you to move to this larger picture of life and love to which we are all called.

Chapter 10
INTO THE FUTURE
Move On!

During this time in human history, our devotion and piety should support, inspire, enhance, and produce a solid framework for social justice activity. Devotional spirituality needs to be linked with a prophetic spirituality in today's society, or it will have nothing authentic to offer the global community. As Franciscan Sister and Theologian Ilia Delio says, "It is time to embrace our new reality; medieval Christianity is bankrupt, Newtonian systems are deadly, and individualism is an illusion."[1] Luke 5:36–39 reminds us that we must create something new to accommodate the new reality that we live in.

A devotional spirituality tends to focus on comfort for the practitioner, while a prophetic spirituality is actively charged with the transformation of self and community. Ideally, the two should work in tandem. The prophetic link is "about awareness, of choice, and of risk. It is about the embrace of life, the pursuit of wholeness, the acceptance of others, and the call to co-creation."[2] Prophetic ministry serves to energize the community by using the imagination—to dream God's kingdom into reality. "The task of prophetic ministry is to nurture, nourish, and evoke a consciousness and perception of the dominant culture around us."[3]

To bring about this dream we must move from and integrate a devotional spirituality (the experience of God's Love) to a prophetic spirituality (the demands of that love). Such a spirituality

- Sees through the lies of the culture
- Is grounded in the Word of God and maintains a holy intolerance for injustice
- Points beyond self to the greater good, the will of God, and the protection of the people
- Is always loud, bold, clear, and nonviolent in proclaiming the truth
- Faithfully and patiently endures the long haul
- Envisions a world in which justice and equality, peace and community are the norm[4]

Sr. Joan Chittister, OSB, summarizes the role of the prophet in our midst: "Prophets...hold the rest of the vision of holiness, the part that seldom is taught in the same breath as charity or morality or good citizenship. They are the other half of Christianity, the forgotten half of the spirituality of the Christian world."[5] Remember this is what we have been baptized into—the prophetic role of Christ, as well as the priestly and royal identity of the Savior. Each of us, according to our life situation, can live out this spirituality in regular practical ways.[6]

In light of this, what would a mature spirituality look like for our time? I believe it would include the following key characteristics: It must be

1. Holistic: body, soul, and spirit
2. Relational: equal, mutual, and reciprocal
3. Immersive: focused and present to reality
4. Transformative: self, community, and society

5. Universal: beyond self to all of creation
6. Mystical: immersed in love
7. Dynamic: active and interactive

What type of devotions and spiritual practices will support you in living out this value system?

In looking at the Wisdom tradition, we can find some spiritual imperatives that will actively provide that support:

1. Live each moment as if it were your last.
2. Count the gifts of the moment.
3. Live without being possessed by need for fame, fortune, power, or popularity.
4. Love without regret.
5. Forgive out of an abundance of goodness.
6. Trust the power of Divine Presence.
7. Pray contemplatively and act justly.
8. Honor creation.

As Pope Francis has said, "Following Jesus is not neutral, following Jesus means being involved, because faith is not a superficial decoration, it is strength of the soul!"[7]

To that end, I suggest that present devotional prayer forms could be reworked for the challenging context of our postmodern society, to help facilitate this proposed value system. "Prophetic spirituality requires us to stop hiding behind a life of prayer as an excuse to do nothing about anything."[8] We must think beyond our own small world to the effects of issues upon others outside our own local area and social setting.

I invite you to research your own favorite devotions to discover their historical background, political influences, and cultic inspirations. In light of your research, what changes would you like to effect to help you make the devotion more impactful for your own spiritual life and more likely to move toward engagement in public life? As a faith community, we could also create new devotions, honoring the history of these traditional prayer forms, while acknowledging the need for new, updated forms of prayer. Here are some ideas:

Saints

1. Choose a saint that you admire. Picture yourself going for a walk with that person. What do you want to discuss? What specifically would you like them to do for you or with you? Pray from the heart using your own words. If this is too challenging, you might find *Prayers from the Heart,* by Richard Foster, or *Guerrillas of Grace: Prayers for the Battle*, by Ted Loder, helpful in getting you started. Both of these books use language that comes from the heart but has a more creative approach.

2. How do you experience the holiness of Christ growing in you? How is God inviting you to reach out to others?

3. You might also find spiritual reading to be very helpful, especially the writings of the saints themselves or of contemporary spiritual leaders. I have found Sr. Joan Chittister to be immensely helpful in this regard. Her book *Radical Spirit: 12 Ways to Live a Free and Authentic Life* is most helpful. For an example of honest, compelling, and no-nonsense conversation with God, you might like to try Australian Jesuit Fr. Richard Leonard's books *Why Bother Praying?* and *Where the Hell Is God?*[9]

4. You might also consider becoming an intercessor for the specific needs of your parish or neighborhood. This could be expanded to regularly praying for, and fasting for, the needs of the Church and our world.

5. Making a pilgrimage to a holy site is a traditional practice of "walking your prayer." I have found this to be an especially meaningful experience. You could choose to travel to the site of your baptism, wedding, the final resting place of a loved one, or the place of your conversion.

6. Enlarge your own life in small and large ways: become a local expert on the issues that trouble your community (e.g., economic inequality, racial discrimination, use of natural resources, neighborhood or family violence, etc.); recycle materials, wear hand-me-down clothes, reasonably ration your use of water, purchase less, and give away what is not being used, in other words, practice a more sustainable diet for the planet.

7. Link small groups together to discuss reading material over coffee or a meal. Work on a project together.

Mary

1. Imagine Mary in all her generosity and compassion. Become centered, clear, and then picture her—her radiance, her compassion, her gentleness. Once the image is complete, allow her to approach you and merge into you, feeling yourself united with her.[10]

2. Pray the Rosary, meditating on the mysteries of your own life: the sorrowful, joyful, luminous, and glorious episodes in your life history. You might also try praying the Rosary by inserting the particular name of the person you want to pray for in the Hail Mary during each decade of the rosary (i.e., ...pray for Lucy now and at the hour of her death. Amen.). You could also use the Ignatian method of transposition as you pray and meditate on the mysteries. Imagine yourself in the specific scene of the mystery (e.g., at the annunciation). Where are you exactly? Are you an observer or a participant in this encounter? What is said?

3. A contemplative praying of the Rosary is much better than praying in a rushed or perfunctory manner.

4. Reflect on the annunciations in your own life. What have you learned? What have you done as a result of these annunciations?

5. Embrace the whole of your life story, even the dark, painful, and mysterious aspects.

6. Actively participate in the work of the Church, either individually or with a particular group.

7. Reflect on your chosen nature. Knowing who you are as God's beloved, how will you live your life?

8. Practice living a simpler life with fewer possessions, perhaps joining a community garden program, or choosing vacations that interface with nature.

9. Meditate on the Scriptures that relate to Mary and then respond as you feel led.

10. Embrace the fullness of your own femininity or masculinity.
11. Questions for meditation prompted by Mary's example:
    a. How is Mary inviting you to embody your own spirit and actively proclaim the good news to others?
    b. How are you being asked to do the will of God?
    c. Are you willing to entrust yourself completely to God's love and plans for you?
    d. Where in your life is God asking you to create something new?
    e. How is God inviting you to care for others?

The Eucharist

1. Choose a part of the eucharistic celebration that you would like to focus on (e.g., the Penitential Rite, Presentation of the Gifts, or Sign of Peace). How would you like to incorporate this action into your life at this time? For the Penitential Rite, you might consider doing a forgiveness novena or forgiving someone in particular. For the Presentation of the Gifts, you might think of an area of your life that you are ready to surrender or offer up to God. The Sign of Peace could be an invitation for you to confront an area in your life where you are in conflict and are not peaceful. Perhaps you are being invited to reconcile with that part of yourself or your relationships.

2. Another possibility is to engage in a *lectio divina* or reflective meditation with the Scripture readings of the day.

3. Begin your meetings or gatherings with a group *lectio divina*. How is Jesus inviting you to open yourself up to God's abiding love?

4. Memorize certain Scripture passages that you can lean on in your times of desolation, for example, I can do all things in Christ who strengthens me (Phil 4:13); Only in God is my soul at rest, from him comes my salvation (Ps 62:1); "There is...now no condemnation for those who are in Christ Jesus" (Rom 8:1).

5. Alternatively, you could commit to do an act of service each week (such as reaching out in love to a neighbor who does not fit comfortably into your social or political viewpoint, or feeding the poor or visiting the sick) as a sign of your desire to put into practice the eucharistic message of nourishment for others.

6. Practice eating mindfully. Live authentically as the Real Presence of Christ on earth. Be present to reality as it is: Do not run from it, deny it, or seek to control it. Accept it!

7. Write letters, emails, or messages via Twitter or the like to your elected representatives or leaders about particular issues that impact the voiceless or disempowered.

8. Another practice that you may find helpful in this regard, if you live in a nonfamilial setting, is to plan, prepare, and eat a meal together with those with whom you live, guided by meaningful questions to deepen your community.

9. Finally, you might discover the wonderful healing gift of a well-planned ritual as a means to transition into a new reality (e.g., moving residences, healing a relationship, moving on after a divorce or death, transforming a traumatic situation, or honoring a loss). Trauma is rarely healed. Rather, it is transformed and can then be carried and integrated into one's life story.[11]

The Passion of Christ

1. Offer up your life, especially the parts of your life that feel unmanageable, to Jesus. Speak openly and honestly. Imagine yourself placing your failures, sins, and shortcomings at the foot of the cross. Receive his forgiveness, his love, and his blessing.
2. Recite the Litany of the Sacred Heart of Jesus or create your own litany, perhaps using the different titles for Jesus (e.g., Jesus, my friend and companion; Jesus, my guide through life; Jesus, my healer and consoler). David Richo has written a helpful book on this topic, titled *The Sacred Heart of the World: Restoring Mystical Devotion to Our Spiritual Life*.
3. Another way to honor this devotion for contemporary times is to meditate on your own body as a vessel of God's presence. You do not need to wait until you are ill to engage in this prayer form. Why not try praying in gratitude for your hands or your lungs or heart? Finally, you can use this prayer form imagining Jesus embracing you or sharing his heart with you.

4. Meditate on the 100 questions that Jesus asked his followers.[12]

5. Create a Stations of the Cross of your own life. Meditate on each of these encounters. What lessons have you learned from these encounters/experiences?

6. Enter the mystery of Christ's life, death, and resurrection by actively engaging these questions: Where is God inviting you to
   a. Take notice of God's presence?
   b. Be grateful?
   c. Grieve and mourn your losses?
   d. Receive new life?
   e. Adjust and transition into something new?
   f. Let go of old attachments, undue compensations, or restrictive thoughts?
   g. Receive a fresh outpouring of the Holy Spirit?

7. Write a letter to Jesus in your journal. Express yourself as honestly as you can and then "listen" to his response. Perhaps you might try an artistic expression of your feelings as a form of prayer. Drawing, dancing, singing, telling a story, or writing a poem can be most helpful for some people. Listening to music can be a form of *audio divina*—meditative reflection.

8. Jesus was not afraid to confront reality on its own terms. What do you need to face in order to move forward more authentically in your life?

9. Jesus would often pray in the midst of creation. Spend some time in nature and notice the details of creation. Simply drink in the beauty. Think about

how you might pay attention or care for nature in a new way.

10. Reflect on the lessons that you have learned from the painful experiences of your life. Pray for the grace to live in the present moment, rather than living in the past. Do not take difficult things personally, knowing that you are loved by God. Remember that behind every loss, death, or trauma is always new life. The cross leads us to the resurrection.

Always remember that as you do this necessary work for your interior life, that good devotions are determined by how well they lead you closer to Christ, to the Scriptures, and to the liturgies of the Church.

If your devotions do this then you will be truly fulfilling the greatest of the exhortations of Jesus: "love one another as I have loved you" (John 15:12).

With this expansive outlook, we get up off our knees and embrace the world with joy!

APPENDIX

Many of us enjoy praying our favorite devotion to such an extent that the familiarity with it no longer moves us forward in the work of transformation. Remember, the purpose of all religious devotion is to connect us to our heart in relationship with God, whether it is through a particular saint, the Virgin Mary, the Eucharist, or the passion of Christ. Here are a few practical examples of how you might work with your own favorite devotions to effect a greater change in your relationship with God. When regularly practiced, these changes will create an attitude of ongoing transformation.

St. Francis of Assisi

St. Francis of Assisi (1181–1226), arguably one of the most popular saints of all time, had a most fascinating story that attracted many people to his side. In a time when people were looking for a simpler Christian message and model of holiness, Francis appeared on the scene. He was a friar, mystic, preacher, and religious founder. He is the patron of Italy, animals, and the natural environment. Francis was fascinated by Jesus and his incarnation, so he became a "second Christ." He loved the Eucharist and sought to become one with creation.

119

Later in life, Francis received the stigmata and gave the Church the idea of the Christmas crèche. He is well known for bringing together material and spiritual reality in his faith journey. His contemplative prayer life fed and nourished his active life of preaching, caring for the poor, and his love of creation.

- Practice praying contemplatively by sitting in silence observing your thoughts or the activity around you with no need to change anything.
- How can you embrace material and spiritual reality within you? Perhaps you could do some gardening or participate in a local cleanup project as a means of reminding yourself that you are a co-creator with God.
- Support those who are trying to address issues arising from our misuse or abuse of the resources of our planet.
- Perhaps you could join the Third Order Franciscans and live out the Franciscan spirituality in your daily life.
- Think about ways you could simplify your life so that you spend more time focusing on what is most essential to you.
- Write your elected representatives about your desire for greater social justice for the oppressed and marginalized members of our society.
- Join Pax Christi and become committed to non-violent attitudes and actions.

Mary

In December 1531, Juan Diego, an Aztec convert to Christianity, had a series of visions of the Virgin Mary requesting that he have a church built in her honor at Tepeyac Hill, in Mexico. Apparitions tend to happen to poor peasants in times of great stress and turmoil, and this devotion has become widespread. Over the years, she has become a national symbol and patron for Mexico. Her popularity is not limited to religious affairs; the Virgin of Guadalupe has played a major role in Mexican nationalism and identity. She is the Patroness of the Americas, and the basilica in Mexico City is a destination for thousands of pilgrims each year.

How could this devotion be transformative for you in practical terms? Here are some possibilities:

- Make a pilgrimage to an important site that represents for you the sacredness of the Divine.
- Create something beautiful that uplifts others.
- Develop and promote a greater respect for women in particular and the feminine in general.
- Find a way to support the education of an underprivileged young person.
- Honor Mary in a special way by mentoring a young woman.
- Learn about one of the more than 20 different cultures in Latin America as a way of celebrating our larger American identity.
- Learn some Spanish as a means of creating the possibility of greater hospitality to those who only speak and/or pray in Spanish. Attend a Eucharist in Spanish.

The Eucharist

One of our most loved saints of recent times, known for her passionate devotion to Jesus in the Eucharist is Mother

(St.) Teresa of Calcutta. She spent countless hours before the Blessed Sacrament, adoring, praying, but most of all, listening to Jesus, who had explicitly called her to her work with the poor.

Her prayer before the Eucharist was the direct impetus for her unswerving commitment to the poor, the sick, and the dying. She knew the absolute necessity of getting up off her knees and going out into the street.

She provides us with an outstanding model for today.

While very few of us can emulate this amazing woman saint, here are some possibilities for your eucharistic devotion:

- Consciously try to listen for the voice of Jesus. To what is he inviting you?
- Ask St. Teresa to accompany you in your adoration, and to open your heart and mind to the call of Jesus.
- Research local religious orders or charitable groups to discover where you might "go out into the streets," or at least support those who do.

The Passion of Jesus

Sr. Maria Faustina Kowolska (1905–38), a Polish mystic, was known to have visions of Jesus's mercy and the afterlife. Out of these experiences, she developed what might be called a spirituality of mercy, complete with a striking image of red and white light flowing out of the heart of Jesus. She often spoke about the sufferings of Jesus that bring about our salvation. There are definite links among national origins, political influences, and cultic faith expressions that induce or shape people's spiritual experiences. These are often adopted by oppressed persons or people who suffer grievously.

Appendix

Whenever we are drawn to a particular devotion or spirituality, it often carries a subconscious message for us. For example, might it mean that God is inviting you to embrace Divine mercy more fully, so that you can be more merciful to others in your attitude and behavior?

- Besides praying the numerous prayers that she recommended, perhaps God is inviting you to put that mercy into an active practice. (For example, let go of judging those who have a different belief system or political affiliation, or reach outside your comfort zone to care for another person.)
- Each day, consciously receive God's mercy into your life.
- Reach out to a stranger with a smile, a kind word, or a listening ear.
- Reflect on actions you could regularly do to become more loveable to your family members and neighbors.
- Forgive yourself for your shortcomings.
- Regularly forgive others who have offended you.
- Fast from gossiping or ridiculing others. Do not make assumptions.

I hope these examples might act as a kind of template, as you reflect on your own favorite devotions and move outward to bring to the world the love, mercy, compassion, and forgiveness you experience in your devotional practice.

NOTES

Chapter 1

1. *Webster's New World Dictionary of the American Language: Concise Edition*, ed. David B. Guralnik (Cleveland: The World Publishing Company, 1964), 207.

2. Robert Sardello, *The Power of the Soul: Living the Twelve Virtues* (Charlottesville, VA: Hampton Roads, 2002), 37.

3. Congregation for Divine Worship and the Discipline of the Sacraments, *Directory on Popular Piety and the Liturgy: Principles and Guidelines* (Boston: Pauline Books and Media, 2002), 13, §4.

4. *Directory on Popular Piety*, 13, §5.

5. *Directory on Popular Piety*, 18, §2.

6. *Directory on Popular Piety*, 24, §12.

Chapter 2

1. Richard Kieckhefer, "Major Currents in Late Medieval Devotion," in *Christian Spirituality: High Middle Ages and Reformation*, ed. Jill Raitt (New York: Crossroad, 1996), 75.

2. Kieckhefer, "Major Currents," 75.

3. Kieckhefer, "Major Currents," 75–76.

4. Kieckhefer, "Major Currents," 101.

5. Kieckhefer, "Major Currents," 76.

6. Kieckhefer, "Major Currents," 77.

7. Kieckhefer, "Major Currents," 81.

8. Kieckhefer, "Major Currents," 83–85.

9. Kieckhefer, "Major Currents," 85.

10. Kieckhefer, "Major Currents," 88.

11. Kieckhefer, "Major Currents," 89.

12. Kieckhefer, "Major Currents," 89.

13. Kieckhefer, "Major Currents," 90.

14. Kieckhefer, "Major Currents," 90–92.

15. Kieckhefer, "Major Currents," 93.

16. Kieckhefer, "Major Currents," 93–94.

17. Kieckhefer, "Major Currents," 94–95.

18. Kieckhefer, "Major Currents," 95.

19. Kieckhefer, "Major Currents," 97.

20. Kieckhefer, "Major Currents," 97.

21. Kieckhefer, "Major Currents," 97–98.

22. Kieckhefer, "Major Currents," 99–100.

23. Kieckhefer, "Major Currents," 98.

24. Louis Bouyer, *Liturgical Piety*, Liturgical Studies I (Notre Dame, IN: University of Notre Dame Press, 1978), 249.

25. Kieckhefer, "Major Currents," 100–101.

Chapter 3

1. Otto Grundler, "*Devotio Moderna*," in *Christian Spirituality: High Middle Ages and Reformation*, ed. Jill Raitt (New York: Crossroad, 1996), 176–77.

2. Grundler, "*Devotio Moderna*," 177–78.

3. Grundler, "*Devotio Moderna*," 178–80.

4. David Tracy, "Recent Catholic Spirituality: Unity amid Diversity," in *Christian Spirituality: Post Reformation and Modern*, ed. Louis Dupre and Done E. Saliers (New York: Crossroad, 1996), 144.

5. Tracy, "Recent Catholic Spirituality," 147.
6. Tracy, "Recent Catholic Spirituality," 149.
7. Tracy, "Recent Catholic Spirituality," 150.
8. Tracy, "Recent Catholic Spirituality," 151.
9. Tracy, "Recent Catholic Spirituality," 153.
10. Tracy, "Recent Catholic Spirituality," 153.
11. Tracy, "Recent Catholic Spirituality," 154.
12. Tracy, "Recent Catholic Spirituality," 154–55.
13. Tracy, "Recent Catholic Spirituality," 156–58.
14. Tracy, "Recent Catholic Spirituality," 160.
15. Tracy, "Recent Catholic Spirituality," 161.
16. Tracy, "Recent Catholic Spirituality," 162–63.
17. Tracy, "Recent Catholic Spirituality," 164.
18. Tracy, "Recent Catholic Spirituality," 165.
19. Tracy, "Recent Catholic Spirituality," 165.
20. Tracy, "Recent Catholic Spirituality," 165.
21. Tracy, "Recent Catholic Spirituality," 166–67.
22. Tracy, "Recent Catholic Spirituality," 167–68.
23. Tracy, "Recent Catholic Spirituality," 170.
24. Tracy, "Recent Catholic Spirituality," 168–70.

Chapter 4

1. Elizabeth A. Johnson, *Friends of God and Prophets: A Feminist Theological Reading of the Communion of Saints* (New York: Continuum, 1998), 49–70.
2. Johnson, *Friends of God*, 94–105.
3. Congregation for Divine Worship and the Discipline of the Sacraments, *Directory on Popular Piety and the Liturgy: Principles and Guidelines* (Boston: Pauline Books and Media, 2002), §212.
4. Johnson, *Friends of God*, 141–62.
5. Johnson, *Friends of God*, 219–43.

Chapter 5

1. Paul VI, Apostolic Exhortation *Marialus Cultis* for the Right Ordering and Development of Devotion to the Blessed Virgin Mary (February 2, 1974), §36, http://www.vatican.va/content/paul-vi/en/apost_exhortations/documents/hf_p-vi_exh_19740202_marialis-cultus.html.

2. Second Vatican Council, "The Blessed Virgin Mary, Mother of God, in the Mystery of Christ and the Church," chap. 8 in Dogmatic Constitution on the Church *Lumen Gentium* (November 21, 1964), §§52–69, http://www.vatican.va/archive/hist_councils/ii_vatican_council/documents/vat-ii_const_19641121_lumen-gentium_en.html.

3. Elizabeth Johnson, *Dangerous Memories: A Mosaic of Mary in Scripture* (New York: Continuum, 2004), 21.

4. Raymond Brown et al., *Mary in the New Testament* (New York: Paulist Press, 1978).

5. Congregation for Divine Worship and the Discipline of the Sacraments, *Directory on Popular Piety and the Liturgy: Principles and Guidelines* (Boston: Pauline Books and Media, 2002), §189.

6. Ronald Rolheiser, workshop notes.

7. David Richo, *Mary within Us: A Jungian Contemplation of Her Titles and Powers* (Berkeley: Human Development Books, 2007), 9.

8. Leonardo Boff, *The Maternal Face of God: The Feminine and Its Religious Expressions*, trans. Robert Barr (San Francisco: Harper and Row, 1987), 218.

9. Boff, *Maternal Face*, 220.

10. Richo, *Mary within Us*, 20.

11. Richo, *Mary within Us*, 20.

12. For those of you who would like to explore a more psychological understanding of Mary and her role in salvation history, see David Richo, *Mary within Us: A Jungian Contemplation of Her Titles and Powers*; Joan C. Engelsman, *The Feminine Dimension of*

the Divine (Wilmette, IL: Chiron, 1987); or Michael P. Carroll, *The Cult of the Virgin Mary: Psychological Origins* (Princeton, NJ: Princeton University Press, 1992).

13. Elizabeth Johnson, workshop notes.

14. Johnson, *Dangerous Memories*, 100–122.

15. Elizabeth Johnson, workshop notes.

16. Elizabeth A. Johnson, *Friends of God and Prophets: A Feminist Theological Reading of the Communion of Saints* (New York: Continuum, 1998), 233–36.

17. Elizabeth Johnson, workshop notes.

18. Elizabeth Johnson, *Truly Our Sister: A Theology of Mary in the Communion of Saints* (New York: Continuum, 2003).

19. Richo, *Mary within Us*, 21.

20. Pax Christi USA, 1987.

Chapter 6

1. Congregation for Divine Worship and the Discipline of the Sacraments, *Directory on Popular Piety and the Liturgy: Principles and Guidelines* (Boston: Pauline Books and Media, 2002), §161.

2. Jim Clarke, *Creating Rituals: A New Way of Healing for Everyday Life* (Mahwah, NJ: Paulist Press, 2011).

3. William J. Bausch, *A World of Stories: For Preachers and Teachers* (Mystic, CT: Twenty-Third Publications, 1998), 210.

Chapter 7

1. John P. Meier, *A Marginal Jew: Rethinking the Historical Jesus*, vol. 3 (New Haven, CT: Yale University Press, 2001).

2. Jose A. Pagola, *Jesus: An Historical Approximation*, trans. Margaret Wilde (Miami, FL: Convivium Press, 2012).

3. Richard Rohr, *The Universal Christ: How a Forgotten Reality Can Change Everything We See, Hope For, and Believe* (New York: Convergent, 2019).

4. Congregation for Divine Worship and the Discipline of the Sacraments, *Directory on Popular Piety and the Liturgy: Principles and Guidelines* (Boston: Pauline Books and Media, 2002), §166.

5. Ronald Rolheiser, *Sacred Fire: A Vision for a Deeper Human and Christian Maturity* (New York: Image, 2014), 286.

6. Julianne Stanz, *Start with Jesus: How Everyday Disciples Will Renew the Church* (Chicago: Loyola Press, 2019), 68–69.

7. Cynthia Bourgeault, *The Wisdom Jesus: Transforming Heart and Mind—A New Perspective on Christ and His Message* (Boston: Shambhala, 2008).

Chapter 9

1. Jane Regan, class notes.

2. Ezra Bayda, *Saying Yes to Life (Even the Hard Parts)* (Boston: Wisdom, 2005), 158.

3. Frank X. Tuoti, *Why Not Be a Mystic: An Irresistible Invitation to Experience the Presence of God Here and Now* (New York: Crossroad, 1995), 150.

4. Ilia Delio, *A Hunger for Wholeness: Soul, Space, and Transcendence* (Mahwah, NJ: Paulist Press, 2018), 31.

5. Thomas Merton, *Cassian and the Fathers: Invitation into the Monastic Tradition*, ed. Patrick F. O'Connell, Monastic Wisdom Series 1 (Kalamazoo, MI: Cistercian Publications, 2005), 179–80.

6. Thomas Merton, "The Inner Experience," published as an edited offprint serialized over eight issues of *Cistercian Studies*, 1983–85.

7. Joan Chittister, *In God's Holy Light: Wisdom from the Desert Monastics* (Cincinnati: Franciscan Media, 2015), 70.

8. Thomas Merton, *Conjectures of a Guilty Bystander* (New York: Image Books, 1989), 152.

9. Thomas Merton, "The Inner Experience," chap. 8.

Chapter 10

1. Ilia Delio, Omega Center, "The Pandemic Mirror," March 23, 2020.

2. Joan Chittister, *The Time Is Now: A Call to Uncommon Courage* (New York: Convergent, 2019), 16.

3. Walter Brueggemann, *The Practice of Prophetic Imagination: Preaching an Emancipating Word* (Minneapolis: Fortress Press, 2012).

4. Chittister, *Time Is Now*, 16.

5. Chittister, *Time Is Now*, 104.

6. Chittister, *Time Is Now*, 38–40.

7. Pope Francis, Angelus, St. Peter's Square, August 18, 2013, http://www.vatican.va/content/francesco/en/angelus/2013/documents/papa-francesco_angelus_20130818.html.

8. Chittister, *Time Is Now*, 40.

9. See the appendix.

10. David Richo, *Mary within Us: A Jungian Contemplation of Her Titles and Powers* (Berkeley: Human Development Books, 2007).

11. Jim Clarke, *Creating Rituals: A New Way of Healing for Everyday Life* (Mahwah, NJ: Paulist Press, 2011).

12. See http://blog.adw.org/2012/02/100-questions-jesus-asked-and-you-ought-to-answer/ (accessed May 21, 2021).

BIBLIOGRAPHY

Benner, David. *Soulful Spirituality: Becoming Fully Alive and Deeply Human*. Grand Rapids, MI: Brazos Press, 2011.

Chittister, Joan. *The Time Is Now: A Call to Uncommon Courage*. New York: Convergent, 2019.

Clarke, Jim. *Soul-Centered: Spirituality for People on the Go*. Mahwah, NJ: Paulist Press, 2015.

Congregation for Divine Worship and the Discipline of the Sacraments. *Directory on Popular Piety and the Liturgy: Principles and Guidelines*. Boston: Pauline Books and Media, 2002.

Cooke, Bernard. *Sacraments and Sacramentality*. Mystic, CT: Twenty-third Publications, 1994.

Crossan, John Dominic. *Jesus: A Revolutionary Biography*. San Francisco: Harper Collins, 1995.

Dupré, Louis, et al. *Christian Spirituality: Post Reformation and Modern*. New York: Crossroad, 1996.

Funk, Mary Margaret. *Tools Matter for Practicing the Spiritual Life*. New York: Continuum, 2007.

Gateley, Edwina. *Psalms of a Laywoman*. California: Source Books, 1981.

Huebsch, Bill. *Rethinking Sacraments*. Mystic, CT: Twenty-third Publications, 1995.

Johnson, Elizabeth. *Dangerous Memories: A Mosaic of Mary in Scripture*. New York: Continuum, 2004.

———. *Friends of God and Prophets: A Feminist Theological Reading of the Communion of Saints*. New York: Continuum, 1998.

Martin, James. *My Life with the Saints*. Chicago: Loyola Press, 2016.

McGinn, Bernard, et al. *Christian Spirituality: Origins to the Twelfth Century*. New York: Crossroad, 1996.

Meier, John P. *A Marginal Jew: Rethinking the Historical Jesus*, 5 vols. New Haven, CT: Yale University Press, 2001.

Nolan, Albert. *Jesus Before Christianity*. Maryknoll, NY: Orbis Books, 1996.

Norris, Kathleen. *Acedia and Me: A Marriage, Monks, and a Writer's Life*. New York: Riverhead Books, 2008.

Pagola, Jose. *Jesus: An Historical Approximation*, trans. Margaret Wilde. Series Kyrios. Miami, FL: Convivium Press, 2012.

Raitt, Jill, et al. *Christian Spirituality: High Middle Ages and Reformation*. New York: Crossroad, 1996.

Richo, David. *How to Be an Adult in Faith and Spirituality*. Mahwah, NJ: Paulist Press, 2011.

Rohr, Richard. *The Universal Christ: How a Forgotten Reality Can Change Everything We See, Hope for, and Believe*. New York: Convergent, 2019.

———. *The Wisdom Pattern: Order, Disorder, Reorder*. Cincinnati: Franciscan Media, 2020.

Rolheiser, Ronald. *Sacred Fire: A Vision for a Deeper Human and Christian Maturity*. New York: Image, 2014.

Tuoti, Frank. *Why Not Be a Mystic? An Irresistible Invitation to Experience the Presence of God—Here and Now*. New York: Crossroad, 1995.